Practice to Deceive

A thriller

Norman Robbins

D1637919

Samuel French — London
www.samuelfrench-london.co.uk

CHARACTERS

Adrian Brookes, late thirties
Mildred McBride, late sixties
Gavin Purdie, forties
Donald Caffrey, about seventy
Jessica Scanlon, early forties
Diana Wishart, twenties
Susan Tonks, slightly older than Diana
Rhoda Bradstock, fifties
Detective Inspector Tyson, male or female, forties
Detective Sergeant Morley, male or female, thirties

SYNOPSIS OF SCENES

The action of the play takes place in the living-room
of the Herdsman's Cottage, McBride's farm, Upper
Chellingford, North Yorkshire.

ACT I
SCENE 1 Late summer, about midday
SCENE 2 A few hours later

ACT II
SCENE 1 Two hours later
SCENE 2 Ten minutes later

Time — the present

COPYRIGHT INFORMATION

(See also page ii)

For Lesley and Rex Darlow
who have both lit up my productions
in their respective ways

Other plays and pantomimes
by Norman Robbins
published by Samuel French Ltd

And Evermore Shall Be So
At The Sign of the "Crippled Harlequin"
Aladdin
Ali Baba and the Forty Thieves
Babes in the Wood
Cinderella
Dick Whittington
The Dragon of Wantley
The Grand Old Duke of York
Hansel and Gretel
Hickory Dickory Dock
Humpty Dumpty
Jack and Jill
Jack and the Beanstalk
The Late Mrs Early
Nightmare
The Old Woman Who Lived in a Shoe
Prepare to Meet Thy Tomb
Prescription for Murder
Pull the Other One
Puss in Boots
Red Riding Hood
Rumpelstiltzkin
Sing a Song of Sixpence
Slaughterhouse
Sleeping Beauty
Snow White
Tiptoe Through the Tombstones
Tom, the Piper's Son
A Tomb with a View
Wedding of the Year
The White Cat
The Wonderful Story of Mother Goose

ACT I

The living-room of The Herdsman's Cottage, McBride's Farm, Upper Chellingford, North Yorkshire. Late summer, about midday

The room is wide, but not of much depth. The back wall consists of two long windows, separated by a stable-door with iron fittings. This can be opened in two halves, or, by sliding a connecting bolt, may operate as a single door. The door leads into a small, leaded windowed, porch, which in turn leads out R into the farmyard. Through the windows can be seen part of the barn opposite. Heavy looking drapes on wooden poles hang at the windows. Beneath each window are oak cabinets. One has a set of drawers, the other holds a collection of drinks bottles and assorted glassware. On top of the cabinets, flower bowls or vases, knick-knacks, etc. Downstage of the wall, R, is a doorless opening that affords a glimpse of the narrow staircase to the upper floor, whilst upstage of this, a Welsh dresser stands, its shelves laden with the remnants of a large dinner service from bygone years. Opposite this, in the wall L, is a door that leads to the kitchen. Below this, almost opposite the stairs, is a large fireplace, circa 1930s. The mantle of this is adorned with various objects, and above this, a framed portrait of an elderly Victorian man. Upstage of the kitchen door is a bookcase. Assorted books and games are on the shelves. Downstage, a rectangular table supports a small television set. A magazine rack is beside this. A comfortable looking sofa is R, positioned just above the opening to upstairs, and angled to face down L. A matching armchair is by the fireplace, angled down R. A small occasional table is close to the upstage arm, and a table lamp stands on this, plus a hard-backed book, its open pages held in place by a pair of reading glasses. The room is carpeted, the walls hold various framed pictures, and though all appears rather dated, it is comfortable and welcoming. Light switches are by the main door, and at the foot of the stairs

When the scene begins, it is a brilliantly sunny day, the room is empty, but the upper part of the stable door is open, as is the kitchen door. In the distance, a dog is barking

A few moments later, Adrian Brookes passes the window R, *and enters the porch. In his late thirties, he wears an open-necked shirt and dark trousers, and carries a large brown envelope containing a studio photograph of a young woman*

Adrian (*calling into the room, uncertainly*) Hello?

There is no reply

   Anybody home?

As no one appears, he exits the porch, and moves back to look L. *A few moments later, he enters the porch and calls again*

   Hello?

There is still no reaction. The barking stops, and after a short hesitation, he opens the lower part of the door and enters the room. Crossing to the kitchen door, he peers inside, then moves to the bottom of the stairs and looks up

   (*Calling*) Hello?

Mildred McBride lumbers past the window R, *and into the doorway. She is a stout, ruddy-faced, no-nonsense woman in her late sixties, wearing farm working clothes and wellington boots. She carries a double-barrelled shotgun*

Mildred (*grimly*) Needing help, are you?
Adrian (*turning to see her*) Mrs Scanlon?
Mildred (*brusquely*) She's not here. And neither should *you* be. Got bad eyes, have you? Didn't you see the board?

Adrian looks at her blankly

   On the gate. No trespassing and no visitors. Especially *your* kind (*Raising the gun*) Now get yourself out of here before I let my finger slip.
Adrian (*raising his hands slightly*) Now just a minute ——
Mildred (*harshly*) Not even a second. And if you've not made it to the gate by the time I count ten, you'll have Boris on your tail. And you'd not like *that*, I can promise you. Teeth like a shark, and doesn't care which bit of you he sinks 'em in. Last one of your lot's still having treatment.

Adrian My lot?

Mildred Reporters. Bloody parasites, the lot of you. If I had my way, there'd be government grants for every one culled. Now move it. (*She motions to the door with the gun*)

Adrian There seems to be some mistake ——

Mildred (*tartly*) Yes. And we both know who's made it.

Gavin Purdie hurries past the window R, *and into the doorway. He is a rough-looking man in his forties, shirtless, heavily tanned and wearing filthy bib-overalls with heavy boots. He speaks with a slight drawl and could appear to be sly or slightly retarded*

Gavin Everything all right, Mrs M? Seen you heading here with Mr's old shotgun. (*He sees Adrian*) Who's this, then?

Mildred (*lowering the gun, slightly*) 'Nother reporter. That's all. Nosing round when he thought the coast were clear. But he's just leaving ... (*to Adrian; pointedly*) ... aren't you?

Adrian If you'd let me get a word in ——

Gavin (*glowering*) You heard what Missis said.

Adrian I'm not a reporter. I've nothing to do with the media. My name's Brookes. Adrian Brookes. And I'm looking for Mrs Scanlon.

Mildred And I've already told you. She's not here.

Gavin Won't be back till ——

Mildred (*cutting in*) *You're* long gone. And the next time you're on my land without invitation, I'll shoot first and ask questions later. Understand?

Adrian (*lowering his hands*) Look ... I don't know who you are, but all I want is a little help, and Mrs Scanlon could be the one to provide it.

Mildred (*flatly*) And why's that?

Adrian Because she's just lost her friend, and I've lost my sister. I've got to know if there's a link.

Mildred and Gavin glance at each other, then she reluctantly lowers the gun completely

Mildred Your sister, you say?

Gavin (*wide-eyed*) Not one of *them* is she? Up on the moor?

Adrian (*relieved*) No, thank God. She's only been missing a few months and according to the *Telegraph*, the last one's been there some years. But not knowing if she's dead or alive is driving me crazy. The only thing I do know, is she's out there somewhere. I'm convinced of it.

Mildred Oh?

Adrian (*explaining*) We used to live in Selwick. Before we moved south.

Mildred (*suspiciously*) You don't sound like a local.

Adrian I'm not. Our parents bought the Selwick house when I was fourteen, but we only stayed three years before heading back to Harrogate. Been there twenty years, now.

Mildred So what's she doing back here, then? Your sister.

Adrian After she vanished, we spent *days* looking for her. Me ... the police ... everybody. But there wasn't a trace. At first they thought she might have had some kind of accident, but some of her clothes and a suitcase were missing ... and the cash she'd kept in a biscuit tin. So when someone came forward who thought they'd seen her getting on a London train, they decided she'd left home deliberately and called off the search. It wasn't till last week, I heard someone answering her description had been seen on Chellingford Moor, apparently living rough. I could have kicked myself for not thinking of it earlier. She knew people in this area. They left her alone. Didn't stare at her.

Mildred Stare?

Adrian (*resignedly*) She has a naevus ... a purple birthmark ... on her left cheek. (*Hastily*) Not as bad as some ... she can hide it fairly well these days with special make-up ... but since Mother died, she's developed a kind of complex about it. Become more sensitive and cut herself off from us. Friends. Family. People she's known for years. When she finally vanished ... well ... (*awkwardly*) we didn't know if we'd see her again. (*Brightening*) But if she's hiding out round here, I can maybe talk some sense into her. Make arrangements for plastic surgery, or something?

Gavin (*frowning*) Bit of a risk, if it is her. Coming back to these parts. Don't she read the papers?

Adrian She was gone before the story broke. And if she is living rough, she probably wouldn't have seen them. Relied more on television. (*Frowning*) But even if she had ... it wouldn't have occurred to her that she might be in danger. She doesn't think that way.

Mildred Not the best place for a woman like her, though. Like the p'lice said. Could be the reason he killed them.

Gavin (*nodding*) Hated deformities, see? One lame, one with fingers missing ——

Mildred (*cutting in*) And what's Jessie got to do with it? Mrs Scanlon, that is?

Adrian Because of her friend ... Mrs Lipton. I read about it at the place I'm staying ... *The Wild Goose*, in Lower Chellingford. She vanished from her home, exactly the way Laura did.

Gavin (*nodding*) Few days ago. And not been seen since.

Adrian She was due here, wasn't she? At this farm. And according to the report, Mrs Scanlon got worried when she didn't turn up, and contacted the police.

Mildred (*flatly*) Hadn't been for the bodies they found last month, they'd never have moved so fast. They'd a team on the moor, next morning.

Gavin (*disgustedly*) Not that they found anything. 'Cept half a dozen camp sites where reporters had been hiding themselves. Looked like rubbish dumps, they said. Bottles and sandwich wrappings, everywhere.

Adrian Anyway ... that's why I'm here. As Mrs Scanlon lives on the moor, I thought there was a chance she could have seen Laura and be able to point me in her direction.

Mildred (*doubtfully*) Shouldn't think that's likely. Them of us lives in these parts don't go tramping round the moor, 'less we're looking for strayed sheep or the like. Too much to do on the farm.

Gavin Besides ... be like tempting fate till they've got him under lock and key, wouldn't it? Good lookin' woman, she is.

Mildred (*dismissively*) You watch your mouth, Gavin Purdie. And get yourself back to the barn. There's all the stuff for Jackson's to sort out before he gets here, and you've wasted enough time already.

Gavin (*abashed*) Right you are, Mrs M ... Only wanted to see you weren't having problems.

Mildred Well now you know.

Gavin exits into the porch, then passes the window to exit R

(*Resting the gun against the chest* R) So. How long you say she's been missing?

Adrian Just over three months. Beginning of June.

Mildred (*looking at him askance*) And you've only just decided she might be in these parts?

Adrian Like I said ... it's twenty years since we moved away. I didn't even *think*. I mean ... She was barely twelve when we left. If it hadn't been for these murders, I'd never have dreamed she could have headed in this direction. It was on the box, you see? Three nights ago. *News at Ten*. They were looking for a possible witness ... a woman with a port wine stain on her cheek ... thought to be living rough on Chellingford Moor. It had to be Laura. It couldn't be anyone else.

Mildred So why not let the p'lice deal with it, 'stead of charging up here yourself?

Adrian She's my sister. And I don't want her ending up as another victim.

Mildred regards him thoughtfully for a moment then indicates the sofa

Mildred You'd better sit down. I'll make us a pot of tea. (*She moves towards the kitchen door*)

Adrian (*surprised*) Mrs Scanlon won't mind?

Mildred (*halting to look at him*) Herdsman's Cottage is mine, so you needn't think I'm taking liberties. The name's McBride. Mildred McBride. Jess only rents it from me. Has for the past four years. Me and Boris keep an eye on it whenever she's away. (*Satisfied*) Nobody gets past *him*, old as he is. Can hear a field mouse in a thunderstorm. Handy, when you're as far from Chellingford as we are. (*She begins to exit again*) Milk and sugar?

Adrian Just milk, please.

Mildred exits into the kitchen

Adrian sits on the sofa, still clutching the envelope

Mildred (*off*) Only you two, is it? You and your sister?

Adrian (*raising his voice*) Elder brother in New Zealand. Eddie. Emigrated six years ago. Just after Mum died.

Mildred (*off*) And what about your father?

Adrian Died in ninety-three.

Mildred appears in the doorway

Mildred So you and her share the house, do you?

Adrian (*shaking his head and resuming normal tones*) No, no. Laura has the house. Becca and I had our own place. In Marlock, about ten miles away.

Mildred That'll be your wife, I take it?

Adrian (*ruefully*) Was. We split up five years ago. Left me for the local Director of Community Services.

Mildred Did you know she was seeing him?

Adrian (*shaking his head*) Hadn't a clue. And it wasn't a him, it was a her.

Mildred (*after digesting this*) Children?

Adrian Us, you mean? No, thank God. I couldn't have coped, bringing them up on my own. (*Wryly*) Though Laura wouldn't have minded. She'd have loved being an auntie. Always wanted a family, though she knew it'd never happen.

Mildred And why's that?

Adrian (*bitterly*) It's not every man who'd see past the outer layer. (*Musing*) I think that's what was getting to her. She even got rid of the mirrors. Couldn't bear to see her reflection. (*Earnestly*) But it wasn't that bad. I mean, yes, you could see it, but there're people with far worse ones. The rest of us hardly noticed it.

Mildred So you never expected her vanishing?

Adrian (*shaking his head*) One day she was there, and the next she'd gone. No note. Nothing.

Mildred (*glancing into the kitchen*) I'll get that tea.

Mildred vanishes from view

Adrian slumps, remaining motionless

Mildred enters with two mugs of tea

There's scones in the tin if you'd like one? (*She hands him a mug*)

Adrian (*putting the envelope beside him and accepting it*) No thanks. I couldn't eat a thing after the breakfast I had.

Mildred moves up to the window R and gazes out

I don't usually bother. (*He sips at the tea*) Never turn down a good cuppa, though.

Mildred (*after a short silence*) I'm not sure I should be telling you this, but you'd hear about it soon enough. They found another one this morning. Out Mullen's Rock way.

Adrian (*slightly thrown*) I'm sorry? (*He suddenly realizes*) You mean ...? (*Stunned*) Oh, my God. (*Beginning to rise*) It wasn't *Laura*?

Mildred (*turning to him*) Shouldn't think so. If she'd anything wrong with her face, the p'lice would have mentioned it.

Adrian subsides again

More recent than the rest, though, according to the one who gave us the news. Wanted Jess to do an identification. Been gone two hours, now. (*She sips at her tea*)

Adrian So that's where she is? Up at Mullen's Rock?

Mildred Or wherever they've taken her.

Adrian (*putting his mug on the floor and rising again*) I'd better get up there. (*He prepares to leave*)

Mildred No point panicking till we know something. She's going to phone if it's good news, but we've heard nothing yet.

Adrian (*uncertainly*) So it could be Mrs Lipton?

Mildred It could. Though I have my doubts. Who'd kill somebody wi' not an enemy in the world? (*She sips at her tea*)

Adrian (*cynically*) Is there anyone that lucky? (*Frowning*) But you may have something. According to the papers, she lives in Tamstock, doesn't she?

Mildred What's that got to do with it? (*She moves down* R *of the sofa*)
Adrian Well ... It's thirty miles or so from here. We used to visit friends
there when we lived in Selwick.
Mildred And?
Adrian (*shrugging*) If she vanished from home, why search for her
here? Unless they thought it was the obvious place after finding all the
others. Five of them, wasn't it?
Mildred (*nodding slightly*) And only two identified. (*Thoughtfully*) But
now you mention it, I wouldn't have thought it an obvious place to
look for her. She were expected here ... Jess were quite excited about
it. Couldn't wait to show her round. But she could have gone anywhere
in the meantime. Like you said, apart from the one they've just found,
the other poor souls had been buried up there for years.

Donald Caffrey passes the window R *and appears in the doorway.*
About seventy, he wears old cord trousers, grubby vest beneath an
open shirt with the sleeves rolled up, and has oil-streaked hands and
arms

Hadn't been for a couple of teenagers looking for a love-nest, they
might have stayed there forever. Not exactly a tourist attraction,
Seddon's Marsh.
Adrian (*remembering*) No.
Mildred Hardly time to get their clothes off before they found the first
one. Heard *her* screaming in Felstone, according to the locals.
Donald (*from the doorway*) You've just missed a call, Millie. Two for
tonight, and one's allergic to cats. Here about six, if that's all right. I
told 'em "yes".
Mildred (*turning to him*) Double or twin?
Donald Didn't say. (*Entering the room*) But it's two women, so I've
pencilled 'em in for the twin. (*He moves down* L, *casually*)
Mildred And how long're they staying?
Donald (*shrugging*) Only mentioned tonight, but there's nothing in the
book for the rest of the week, so you can sort it out with 'em when they
arrive. (*To Adrian*) Yours the new Citroën, back of the stables?
Adrian Yes.
Donald (*nodding*) Might like to move it, then, afore old Jackson arrives
with his van. Eyesight's not what it used to be, and he's none too
particular at the best of times. Hadn't been for his lad, he'd have
backed into the p'lice car last time he came. Lucky they was both in
the house and didn't see. (*Frowning*) Don't I know you?
Adrian (*doubtfully*) I wouldn't think so.
Donald (*dredging his memory*) Not one of the Endicotts, are you? Ran
the newsagents, Selwick way. Back in the nineteen-eighties. Girl and

two boys, they had. Remember 'em kicking a ball 'round that little patch of grass by the shop when I called to pay my bill each week. Them, and another lad. Hair like a kitchen mop, he had. Wonder he could see where he was going.

Adrian (*surprised*) That was me. Adrian Brookes. I used to meet up with the Endicotts every Saturday morning to catch the bus into Chellingford.

Donald (*triumphantly*) Thought you looked familiar. (*Remembering*) Henry and Kathleen's boy. (*He beams happily*) Not often I forget a face.

Adrian Even after twenty years. (*Admiringly*) I'm impressed. Very impressed.

Mildred (*drily*) He might have a memory for faces, but not for much else. If I wasn't here to remind him ten times a day, the place'd be going to rack and ruin. (*She finishes her tea*)

Donald (*grinning*) Nothing wrong with my mind, Millie. (*To Adrian*) Been living and working here since her husband died in ninety-three, but can still name most folks in Selwick.

Adrian So you used to live there, Mr —— ?

Donald Caffrey. Don Caffrey. (*He grins*) Millie's right hand man.

Mildred throws him a dirty look

No, no. Not in Selwick, itself. I'd a cottage on Ted Rowland's farm ... Windy Ridge ... just off the Chellingford Road. (*He grimaces*) All gone now. Idiot planners gave permission to turn it into one of they so-called business parks, and now it's covered wi' concrete, glass an' God knows what else, and bugger-all use to anybody. Half the building's been empty since the day it opened. But you'll know that, won't you?

Adrian (*apologetically*) Afraid not.

Mildred (*cutting in*) He doesn't live there, now. They moved away twenty years ago.

Donald (*puzzled*) So ... ?

Mildred He's back here looking for his sister. She's gone missing and he thinks she could be up on the moor.

Donald (*concerned*) Not one of *them*?

Mildred (*sharply*) 'Course not, you fool. She's only been gone a few months. *They*'ve been up there since the nineties.

Donald (*objecting*) And what about the new one? Her they found this morning?

Mildred (*firmly*) Nothing to do wi' them, in my opinion. And it can't be the same killer, can it?

Adrian (*curiously*) Why not?

Mildred Because if they've been there for years, why would he stop, and start killing again now?

Adrian (*quietly*) How do they know he stopped? There could be dozens up there they haven't a clue about. It's a big moor.

Donald (*shaking his head*) Millie's right. If he's got away with it this long, he'd be mad to stir things up wi' the p'lice still hovering round. (*Remembering*) And besides ... there was nothing wrong with Jess's friend, was there? She said so.

Mildred Nothing she knew of. But if ——

The dog begins to bark again and she and Donald exchange glances

Could be Jess, now.

Donald Or Gus Jackson. He did say he might come early.

Adrian I'd better move my car.

The barking stops

Donald (*raising his hand to stop him*) No. It's all right. It's not Gus. Can't stand the sight of him, old Boris. (*Grinning*) Thinks he's robbing us blind when he's loading up the van. Barks non-stop till they're out of sight again. I'd best take a look, though. Could be folks wanting bed and breakfast.

Mildred (*balefully*) Or more reporters. If word's got out about the new body, they'll be buzzing round again like flies on a cow-pat. (*Putting her mug on the window-ledge and picking up the gun*) I'll see to this. You get back to the tractor. Or have you finished, yet?

Donald 'Nother ten minutes and it'll be good as new.

Mildred (*tartly*) Well make it quick, and then you can help Gavin. If he gets any slower he'll be competing with Chellingford Planning Department.

Mildred exits briskly

Donald (*grinning*) Make a good team, her and old Boris. Both got barks worse than their bites. (*He settles himself on the chair arm*) So. What's this about your sister gone missing? (*He indicates for Adrian to sit again*)

Adrian (*sighing*) Walked out three months ago and hasn't been seen since. (*He sits on the sofa again*) But the police appealed for a potential witness to come forward after those bodies were found on the moor, and the description fits her like a glove.

Donald (*shaking his head*) Wouldn't want any of mine up there if I had 'em. Nasty business. Shows how things change, doesn't it? Scarce ever off the place when I was a lad. Broke a leg once, falling off Mullen's Rock, and took 'em till next day to find me. Didn't put me off, though. Soon as I could get about, I was up there again. Knew I was safe, see? Not like the kids today. Folks are scared to let them out of their sight.

Adrian (*protesting*) But it's been safe up to now. Before they found the bodies. I used to spend *hours* up there when I lived in Selwick.

Donald Twenty years ago, yes. But like I said. Times change. Been two or three tragedies in recent years. Lad from Felstone Primary found in the old quarry with his neck broke. Twin girls drowned in Seddon's Marsh, and a fourteen-year-old black boy beaten up by his own schoolmates, covered in white paint and left tied to a tree, stark naked, in the middle of Hammond's Copse. (*He sighs heavily*) Makes you wonder what the world's coming to. (*Remembering*) But you were telling me about your sister. Can't seem to place her. Though I must have seen her round the place.

Adrian (*shrugging*) She didn't get into the village much. Because of the ... (*Indicating with a twiddling finger*) ... naevus. Made her a bit on the shy side till she got to know folks. Happier with her pets. You might have seen her with Eddie, our elder brother. Followed him round like a dog ... much to his disgust. (*Smiling*) I think it cramped his style.

Donald (*shaking his head*) Don't have a photo, do you?

Adrian Yes, as a matter of fact. (*He shows him the envelope*) I brought it along to show Mrs Scanlon.

Jessica Scanlon passes the window R, *followed closely by Mildred, minus the gun. In her early forties, she is dressed in a short-sleeved blouse, denim jeans and sensible shoes. Her shoulder-length hair is casual looking, and she wears little make-up. At the moment, she appears upset, rather unsteady, and clutches a crumpled handkerchief with which she occasionally dabs at her eyes*

Donald (*seeing her pass*) And speak of the devil ... (*He rises hastily*)

Jessica stumbles into the room and makes for the sofa. Adrian hastily rises and backs R

Mildred (*heading for the kitchen*) I'll put the kettle on. Sit yourself down.

Mildred exits into the kitchen

Jessica sits heavily on the L *end of the sofa and bursts into tears*

Donald (*gently*) I take it it *was* her?

Jessica nods and continues crying

Adrian (*to Donald, embarrassed*) I'd better go.

Mildred enters

Mildred Be ready in a few seconds. Water was still warm. (*She bustles to Jessica's side*) Are you sure there's no mistake? It definitely *was* her?

Jessica (*nodding and trying to control herself*) I recognized her straight away. Not her face, of course. It was too badly damaged. But the dress she was wearing. It's the one she wore on the cruise last year. I'd know it anywhere. (*She loses control again*)

Mildred (*soothingly*) There, there, love. (*She kneels beside her*)

Jessica (*sobbing*) Oh, Millie. I've never seen a body before. Especially one like that. (*Angrily*) How could he have done that to her? What could she have felt? (*She continues sobbing*)

Mildred (*glancing round at Donald*) Don't stand there gawping. See if the tea's ready. And put plenty of sugar in it.

Donald hurries into the kitchen

Adrian (*apologetically*) I'll make myself scarce.

Jessica looks up and notices him for the first time

Jessica (*fighting tears back*) Who are you?

Mildred (*firmly*) Just someone who wanted to talk to you, love. But he can do it later. When you've got over your shock.

Jessica (*blankly*) Talk to me? (*She sniffles*) What about?

Mildred Nothing that can't wait.

Jessica (*agitated*) But who is he? I want to know.

Adrian Adrian Brookes, Mrs Scanlon. And as Mrs McBride says, I can call back later. It's nothing important.

Jessica (*to Mildred*) He's not a reporter, is he?

Mildred (*rising*) You know my views on that kind of vermin. If he had been, he'd never have got his foot through the door. Boris'd have had him for breakfast.

Donald enters carrying a mug of tea

Now just sit there and drink your tea while I show him out.

Jessica (*pulling herself together*) No. Wait. (*She dabs at her eye*) I'd sooner do it now. Anything to take my mind off Etta. All I can see is ...

(*She breaks off and looks at Adrian*) What is it you want to talk about? And if it's insurance, or double glazing, you'd better know now, I'm not exactly in a receptive mood. (*She mops at her eyes again and wipes her nose*)

Mildred takes the mug from Donald and hands it to Jessica

Adrian (*nodding*) I know. I wouldn't have blundered in if I'd thought anything like *this* would happen. It was just ... well ... you were my only hope and I feel terrible landing on your doorstep, the way things are.

Jessica (*sniffling*) It might help if I knew what you were talking about.

Donald (*helpfully*) His sister's gone missing.

Jessica looks from Donald to Adrian

Mildred (*glaring at Donald*) I thought you'd got work to do?

Donald I'll finish off later. Can't leave the lass on her own. She's in no fit state.

Mildred And who made you the local consultant? She's not on her own. I'm here, and if she needs any looking after, I'll do it.

Jessica (*to Adrian; puzzled*) But how can I help?

Adrian I was hoping you'd seen her. Up on the moor.

Jessica (*bewildered*) Why should I? I mean ... I don't even know her. (*Quizzically*) Do I?

Adrian (*hastily*) No, no. Of course not. It's just that ... well ... I've brought a photo of her (*he opens the envelope and extracts a large photograph*) and thought it might jog your memory. (*He hands her the photo*)

Jessica (*taking it without looking at it*) Why me?

Adrian Because the local paper said you lived here ... on the edge of the moor.

Jessica (*baffled*) Lots of people live by the moor.

Adrian But not watercolour artists. That's what you do, isn't it? The reporter mentioned it. And living on the moor ... well ... it's obvious you'd be a regular visitor. So there was always the chance you'd seen her while looking for inspiration.

Jessica (*mopping her eyes*) I don't do landscapes, Mr Brookes. Most of my paintings are of animals.

Donald (*nodding*) Did a nice one of Millie's prize ram. And old Boris. Got him on the wall in my room.

Mildred (*to Jessica*) Drink your tea, love. It'll be getting cold.

Jessica (*taking a small sip, and looking at the photograph*) She's very attractive.

Mildred peers at it from beside her

Adrian Takes after Mum. (*Ruefully*) If it hadn't been for the naevus ...
(*Blurting*) You can't see it there, of course. He did a marvellous job
with the lighting and things. And she didn't want it taking, anyway, so
she was hardly co-operative. But Mum insisted and he got the angle
spot on. You honestly wouldn't know, would you?
Jessica (*still looking at it*) She must have been delighted with it.
Adrian (*shaking his head*) Hated it, to be honest.

Jessica looks surprised

Reminded her of what she could have looked like.
Jessica (*quietly*) Yes. (*Sniffling and trying to hold back tears*) Well I'm
sorry I can't help. I've never seen her before in my life. (*Holding out
the photograph to him*)
Donald Mind if I take a look? (*He moves to take it*)
Mildred (*glowering at him*) What for? You've not been up there for
months. How could you have seen her?
Donald (*patiently*) I'm trying to remember what she looked like. I could
have seen her when they lived in Selwick.
Mildred And how'll that help find her? (*Impatiently*) Get yourself back
and finish that tractor. You can call in the barn on the way, and see if
Gavin's still on his feet and working. If he's not got it sorted before
Jackson arrives, you can tell him he'll have my boot up his backside
and he'll be looking for another job.

*Adrian takes back the photo and replaces it in the envelope. Jessica
takes another small sip, then puts her mug down on the floor*

Donald (*sighing deeply*) Right you are, Millie. (*To the others with a
grin*) Like slave labour, this is. All she needs is a whip.
Mildred (*tartly*) I don't need a whip for the likes of you, Don Caffrey.
I can mark *you* wi' the sharp edge of my tongue.
Donald (*archly*) Promises, promises. (*To Jessica*) I'll see you later, Jess.
And I'm real sorry about your friend. If there's anything I can do ...

Mildred glares at him

Donald quickly exits into the farmyard

Mildred (*to Adrian*) Well you've got your answer. She can't help you.
And as you can see, she's in no condition for any more questions, so
I'll see you out.

Adrian Yes. Yes. Of course. (*To Jessica*) I'm sorry to have bothered you.

Jessica (*nodding dully*) I hope you find her.

Adrian (*to Mildred; awkwardly*) No need for an escort. I can make my own way back. Nice to have met you. I just wish ... well ... it had been in different circumstances.

Adrian exits into the farmyard and vanishes from view

The moment he is gone, Jessica bursts into tears again

Mildred Now, now. (*She hastily sits beside her*) It won't bring her back, you know. And they'll soon find out who did it.

Jessica (*sobbing*) But her face. Her poor, poor face. There was nothing left but ... (*She is unable to say the word and sobs again*) Why would anyone do that?

Mildred Hoping she'd not be identified, I suppose. (*Frowning*) And you're sure it was her? You couldn't be mistaken?

Jessica (*almost angrily*) Of course it was her. I've known her for years. I recognized her dress. I told you. She wore it on the cruise. Poor, poor Etta. (*She sobs even louder*)

Mildred bites her lip, uncertain of what to do. Glancing down, she sees the mug of tea near Jessica's feet

Mildred You've hardly touched that tea. (*She picks it up and rises*) I'll make you a fresh one, shall I? It'd do you the world of good. (*She heads for the kitchen door*)

Jessica (*tearfully*) Red poppies and white daisies.

Mildred drops the mug

Mildred (*recovering herself*) Damn. I'd best get a cloth.

She hurries into the kitchen

Jessica continues sobbing. Boris begins barking again

Mildred enters with a cloth, kneels and mops at the floor

Sorry about that. Can't *think* how it happened. More upset than I thought, I expect. I've some carpet cleaner if it happens to show, but I think I caught it quick enough. (*Attempting levity*) And it wasn't one of your best mugs. (*She picks up the mug, or pieces, and stands*)

Boris stops barking

Would you like me to call Dr Harris? See if he can give you something.
They shouldn't have dropped you off and left you to fend for yourself.
Not in the state you're in. Typical police. Once you've served your
purpose, they couldn't give a damn.

Jessica (*pulling herself together again*) They didn't bring me back.
They offered, but I told them I'd walk home. I needed to get some
air.

Mildred (*frowning*) You didn't come over the moor?

Jessica nods

(*Amazed*) And they let you? With a bloody mad-man roaming round
loose?

Jessica (*forcing a smile*) He'd hardly attack me in broad daylight.

Mildred (*sharply*) They'd still no business leaving you on your own.
God knows they do little enough in the first place. (*Calming*) Still ...
now you are here safe, we'll make sure you stay that way. Shall I call
Dr Harris, or not?

Jessica (*shaking her head*) I think I'll lie down for a while. Try to stop
shaking. (*Struggling*) I can't believe I'll never see her again. It's like
losing a limb. I've known her all my life.

Mildred Well you get yourself upstairs, and I'll make a fresh pot of tea.
If you've dropped off before I get there, I'll not disturb you. You need
all the rest you can get. It's a terrible thing, shock, is. When I heard
about my husband ... well ... I know just how you must be feeling.

Jessica smiles wanly, rises, and exits up the staircase

As she vanishes from view, Mildred sags

(*Almost in a whisper*) Red poppies. And white daisies.

*Pulling herself together, Mildred exits into the kitchen with the cloth
and mug*

As she does so, Gavin passes the window, R, and enters the room

Gavin (*looking around*) You here, Mrs M? Got a woman at the house,
looking for lodgings.

Mildred enters

Mildred Can't Donald deal with it? Way he struts about the place, anybody'd think he owned it.

Gavin Haven't seen hair nor hide of him for the last few minutes. P'raps gone up to the top barn. Not finished the tractor though. Bits are all over the place. Bradstock, the name is.

Mildred (*thrown at the change of topic*) What?

Gavin Her at the house. Bit of all right, as well. Old Boris was licking her hand off when I got there. Reckon he's found himself a new friend.

Mildred (*snorting*) Yes, and cows can fly. (*Suspiciously*) What were *you* doing up there? Is all the stuff for Jackson ready?

Gavin All stacked up and waiting. And I only went up to see what dog was making a fuss about. Knewd it weren't him, 'cause I never heard the van. You can hear *that* coming a mile off. Thought it was Jessie's friend finally turned up.

Mildred (*bluntly*) She has. She's just got back from identifying her.

Gavin (*very interested*) Not her they found this morning?

Mildred (*tartly*) How many more do you think they've found? (*She begins to exit into the farmyard*)

Gavin (*catching at her arm and stopping her*) Good question. (*Slyly*) Might be more up there than they realize.

Mildred (*scowling and freeing herself*) And what's that supposed to mean?

Gavin Quite a size, that moor. Bodies could be tucked away all over the place and nobody'd know where to look for 'em. (*He grins nastily*)

Mildred (*irritated*) They'll know where to find yours if you don't get out of the way, and let me deal with the customer.

She exits and lumbers off R

Gavin (*to himself*) 'Cept them who's put 'em there, of course. *They*'d know, all right. Oh, yes. They'd know all right. (*He smiles knowingly*)

The scene ends in a slow fade

SCENE 2

The same. A few hours later

The room is as before, but the two mugs used in the previous scene have been removed. After a moment, Diana Wishart appears outside the window R. She is in her twenties, and dressed for summer in well-worn denim jeans and a shirt

The day has taken a turn for the worse, and the bright sunlight has been replaced with overcast skies. As the scene progresses, the room gets darker

Diana (*calling as she moves towards the open door*) Round here, Sue. This looks more promising.
Susan (*off; distantly*) But he said to turn right.
Diana (*calling back* R) And we did, didn't we? But you saw the notice. Who advertises bed and breakfast, then sticks a board up telling visitors they're not welcome?

Susan Tonks appears outside the window, R. She is slightly older than her friend, but similarly dressed and pulls a wheeled suitcase behind her

No. This must be the place. (*She enters the porch and appears in the doorway*) Hello? Anybody home?

There is no response, so she enters, leaving Susan on the doorstep

Hello? (*She moves to the kitchen door and looks inside*)
Susan (*nervously*) Di, you *shouldn't*.
Diana (*turning to her*) Shouldn't what?
Susan (*plaintively*) Walk into someone's house.
Diana (*pityingly*) Well it's not exactly chained and padlocked, is it? And we *have* booked.
Susan (*earnestly*) It might be the wrong farm.
Diana (*witheringly*) So they borrowed the other one's sign and stuck it outside, did they? We're actually Fanny Hill's farm, but we thought McBrides Farm had a nicer ring to it. Is that what you're saying?
Susan (*protesting*) Of course it isn't. But if we're expected, where is everyone? It's like the Marie Celeste.
Diana (*patiently*) Well it's obviously a working farm. They're probably out milking cows or feeding chickens. (*Impatiently*) Oh, don't stand

out there like Little Orphan Annie. Come in, and we'll sit down till someone turns up.

Reluctantly, Susan enters with the case

It's our fault for being early, I suppose. I did say six o' clock, and it's barely four, now. But it's no use roaming round the moor if it's going to be bucketing down, and I don't like the look of those clouds. (*She sits in the armchair*) Hmm. This is comfy.

Susan (*hopefully*) We could wait in the car.

Diana   And get soaked to the skin dashing back here? Dream on, ducky.

Susan   It might not rain. It wasn't forecast.

Diana   Believe you me, sweetie. The teeniest suspicion of rain, and the moor'll be awash with it. That or fog. Or snow, for that matter. Don't you know your Sherlock Holmes?

Susan looks at her blankly

(*In creepy tones*) *The Hound of the Baskervilles*? (*She growls*)

Susan   (*ignoring this*) And what if it's raining tomorrow?

Diana   There's macs and boots in the car, and a fishing umbrella on the back seat. But rain's one thing, and a deluge is another. Those clouds are definitely delugeous, dear Watson, so we can afford to give it another day. After all ... if we keep our mouths shut, no one'll be suspicious.

Susan   (*moving down and perching on the sofa*) Do we have to do this, Diana?

Diana   Of course we do. How else can I make a name for myself? We're a month behind the rest of them, already.

Susan   (*unhappily*) It's just that it seems so ... tasteless.

Diana   Well, of course it does. Tasteless is what the public wants. (*Seriously*) Look at *Big Brother* and most of the other reality shows on TV. They're about as wholesome as a dog turd, but the companies have made a fortune out of them, haven't they? And why? Because the general public are too stupid to appreciate well-written, intelligent programmes and prefer being titillated by moronic nobodies who can't say their own name without cursing in the middle of it, and make "sordid" sound like God-given talent. They'll lap up something like this, as though they'd won the lottery.

Susan   (*uncomfortably*) I still don't like it.

Diana   Just think of it as *Midsomer Murders*, and I'll be Inspector Barnaby. In any case ... all you have to do is take the photos. I'll be doing the writing.

There is a distant rumble of thunder

Susan (*unhappily*) But it feels wrong. And I'm sure the police won't like it.

Diana (*exasperated*) Won't like what? It's a month since they found the bodies. Half the locals must have been up there by now. All eager to get a first hand look at the crime scene so they could boast about it to their relatives. And how would they know we'd been near the place? A few quick shots, and we'll be heading back here, just a couple of innocent city girls having a stroll on the moors, without a care in the world.

Susan They'll know when the book comes out.

Diana (*firmly*) By which time, it'll be too late for them to do anything about it. (*Pleading*) Oh, come on, Sue. You know how much I need this. A second book's always more difficult than the first. Any writer will tell you that. And besides ... I've already blown the advance, paying off my student debts. Something like this could set me up for life.

Susan I don't see how. I liked your Julia Wallace one, but that was a famous murder. They don't even know who these women are. How can you write a book about them? (*Suddenly*) It's her, isn't it? You're hoping one of them's her.

The thunder sound again. A little closer

Diana (*stung*) Of course I'm not. She couldn't possibly be one of them. They've been buried up there ten years at least, according to the BBC, and she's only been gone four. I'd just left uni, if you remember? And besides ... there was nothing wrong with her. No deformities. Nothing.

Susan It's disabilities or differently abled.

Diana (*blinking*) What is?

Susan (*primly*) Deformities. We don't use that word, these days. It's not politically correct.

Diana (*scornfully*) Bugger political correctness. (*Firmly*) The point is, if she wasn't (*she does air quotations*) "differently abled", why would he have killed her?

Susan Then what are we doing here? There's lots of other murders you could write about. Why does it have to be these?

Diana (*sighing*) I told you. If you want to write best-selling non-fiction crime in this day and age, it's no use writing anything that needs intelligence to read it. It's got to be cheap, tacky, sensational and sexy. My editor said so.

Susan (*unconvinced*) In that case, I'd change editors.
Diana (*resignedly*) It's not that easy when you're as far down the pecking list as I am.

Donald passes the window R, and enters the porch. He is now somewhat tidier than before

(*Suddenly annoyed*) But what a rotten thing to say. I loved Aunt Gerry. She's the last person I'd want to find in a grave.

Donald enters the room

Donald (*gruffly*) If it's bed and breakfast you're after, you're in the wrong place. This is private.

Susan and Diana quickly stand

Should have took the right turn for the house. Down the drive and opposite the big barn.
Diana Mr McBride? (*She holds out her hand*) Diana Wishart. (*She indicates Susan with her head*) And Susan Tonks.
Donald (*ignoring the hand*) Jack's dead. Widow runs the place, now. Nipped into town for a bit of shopping, 'bout an hour ago.
Diana (*smiling*) That explains it, then. (*She lowers her hand*) There was no one in when we arrived and the door was locked.
Donald (*surprised*) Locked?
Diana It wouldn't open, anyway. We rang the bell, several times.
Susan That's why we came round here. To see if we'd made a mistake.
Diana And as this one was open, we came in to wait.
Donald (*frowning*) You didn't see Mrs Bradstock, then?
Diana The owner of this place?
Donald (*shaking his head*) One of the other guests. Said she was staying in for the rest of the day, so she'd keep an eye on the place. Must have gone out after all and locked the door behind her. Surprised you didn't have Boris on your heels. Barks loud enough to wake the dead.
Susan (*brightening*) A dog? We didn't see a dog, did we, Diana? I love dogs. What kind is he?
Donald (*ignoring this*) Good job I spotted your car. Last thing we need is Mrs S to wake up and find strangers in her living-room.
Diana You mean ... there's someone here? Upstairs?
Donald Had a nasty shock a few hours ago, and having a sleep to get over it. If you bring your case, I'll see if we can fix you up. It'll have to

be a double, though. 'Nother couple of women pipped you to the twin beds, 'bout half eleven this morning. (*She turns to exit*)

Susan (*hastily*) That'll be us. That's when we phoned. From the motorway car park.

There is a very loud crack of thunder which startles them all

Donald Best get you over there before the heavens open. Should have had coats with you.

Diana (*taking the suitcase handle*) We've got some in the car.

Donald Weren't expecting you till later. Made better time than you thought, eh? Just as well. You'd not want to be driving if this lot comes down.

Jessica's voice is heard off R

Jessica (*off, calling*) Donald? Is that you?

Donald (*calling*) 'S'all right, Jess. Just dropped by to see you didn't need nothing.

Jessica appears from upstairs, looking tousled and unsteady

Jessica (*muzzily*) I think the thunder woke me.

She switches on the lights and as the room brightens, sees the two women and reacts

Donald (*easily*) Just a couple of ladies booked in at the farm. Came round here by mistake. I'll see them over and be right back.

Jessica Has anyone phoned?

Donald Not so far as I know. Been up in top field till now. I'll check the machine and see, when I open up. Millie's popped into town and looks like the other visitor's gone out and locked up behind her.

Susan (*apologetically*) We didn't mean to intrude. The notice on the gate said "No Visitors", so we came the wrong way.

Donald (*shaking his head*) One of Millie's ideas. Told her it didn't make sense, but she wouldn't listen. Should have taken it down again, the minute they'd cleared.

Diana Gypsy problems?

Susan (*firmly*) She means travellers.

Donald No bother with gyppos on this farm. Boris'd see 'em off before they'd time to think about turning in, and t' bull takes care of Long

Meadow. Don't like intruders, old Clarence. Put him and a caravan face to face, and I know which one I'd put my money on. No. It were put there to keep reporters out. Not paying guests.

Susan Reporters?

Jessica (*tiredly*) When the bodies were found last month.

Diana (*in pretended surprise*) Bodies? (*Pretending to remember*) Oh. Those awful murders, you mean? But surely that was miles away. The other side of the moor.

Jessica Eight by road, but only two and a half if you don't mind walking the moor.

Donald Buggers were crawling over it, following day. Couldn't move for 'em, down here. Ringing the bell and asking questions, dawn till dusk, till Millie got her shotgun out and turned old Boris loose. Soon cleared 'em then.

Diana But why here?

Donald Nearest farm to where they found 'em, I expect. Wanted to know if we'd seen owt suspicious. "How the hell could we?" I told 'em. "We've not got eyes like telescopes. And if they've been up there for years, how're we expected to remember? It's a farm and we've better things to do than looking out for something "suspicious." (*In disgust*) Not got the brains they were born with.

Diana (*innocently*) It must have given you a shock, though. When the news broke. Five bodies, wasn't it?

Donald (*without thinking*) And a fresh one found this morning.

Jessica looks stricken

Jess, here, had to identify her. (*He suddenly realizes what he has said and looks at Jessica in dismay*)

Diana (*eagerly*) You knew her?

Jessica is rigid

Donald (*aghast*) I'm sorry, Jess. I wasn't thinking.

Jessica (*fighting for control*) Yes. I ... I knew her. She was a friend of mine.

Susan (*sympathetically*) How awful.

Jessica (*almost dream-like*) He battered her head in till you couldn't see her face. But I'll be seeing it in my mind for as long as I live. (*She stumbles to the sofa and sits*) Poor, poor Etta.

Donald (*hastily*) I'll see 'em to the house.

Diana (*ignoring him*) Was that her name, then? Etta?

Susan (*incredulously*) Diana.

Jessica (*dully*) Short for Margaretta. But I always called her Etta. Right back to school days. (*She appears to drift off into the past*)

Donald (*getting hold of the suitcase handle and preparing to leave*) I'll take your case, shall I?

Diana releases it

Jessica (*in detached tones*) She was widowed. In a car crash. He was well insured, but the company wouldn't pay out because of some technicality or other, so she had to sell up and move to Tamstock. (*Bitterly*) All those years of handing over money and for what? Absolutely nothing. If they'd written her a cheque, she'd still be alive.

Diana (*tartly*) Pity you can't sue them. But that's insurance companies. They'll happily take your money, but when it comes to making a claim, they'll use every excuse under the sun to avoid paying out. I had an aunt, once, who ——

Susan (*sharply*) Diana. She doesn't want to know that. (*Pointedly*) And we're keeping this gentleman waiting.

Donald (*glancing at the window*) Too late, now. It's started. You'll be soaked to the skin by the time we get there.

Diana (*flippantly*) Well I'm sure we won't dissolve. And a drop of rain never hurt anyone.

Jessica (*pulling herself together*) Why don't you wait here? Until it stops. I could make a pot of tea. Or coffee if you like? I know I want one.

Susan (*embarrassed*) Oh, we couldn't ——

Diana (*quickly*) Of course we could. We weren't expected till six, and it's nowhere near that, yet. (*To Donald*) And when Mrs McBride gets back, you can always tell her where we are, can't you?

Donald (*uneasily*) I suppose so.

Jessica (*reassuringly*) It's all right, Donald. I'll be glad of the company.

Donald If you're quite sure?

Jessica nods and he reluctantly enters the porch, taking the case. Jessica turns away and appears to drift off again

(*To Susan*) I'll turn a few lights on so you don't miss your footing.

Donald hurries into the rain and past the window R, to vanish from view

Diana (*brightly*) Would you like me to draw the curtains? I know it's early, but it's black as pitch out there, and I'm sure you don't want to watch that lot coming down.

There is no reaction from Jessica, so Diana closes the curtains, then moves to the stable-type door and closes both sections of it

There. That's much better. (*To Susan*) Well sit down, Sue. You're like a spare ... guest at a wedding.

Susan glares at her, then moves downstage to sit in the armchair. Diana crosses to the sofa and sits L of Jessica

(*Gently*) It must have been an awful shock. Having to identify her.
Jessica (*snapping out of it*) Hmm? (*She stares at Diana as though she's never seen her before*)
Diana An awful shock. Seeing your friend.
Jessica Yes. (*More firmly*) Yes. (*Forcing a smile*) I'll make that tea, shall I?
Diana (*hastily*) You needn't bother on our account. We're much more concerned about you. (*To Susan*) Aren't we, Sue?

Susan glowers and ignores her

(*To Jessica*) I mean ... I'm trying to imagine how you felt.

Jessica looks at her oddly

I've been dreading the day they might ask me to do it, because I don't think I could. If there's one thing I can't stand, it's the sight of blood.
Jessica (*nodding tiredly*) I'm the same way ... but fortunately there wasn't much. Just ... (*She is unable to continue, closes her eyes, lowers her head and shakes it*)

Diana glances at Susan who glares back

Diana (*to Jessica, gently*) Had you known her a long time?
Jessica (*after a moment*) All my life. We grew up together. Went to school. On holidays. Even chased the same boys. (*She forces a smile*) I was there at her wedding ... and John's funeral, following the crash. They were going to be so happy, then everything went horribly wrong. (*She almost breaks down, but struggles back*) She'd no other family, and being on her own with no income or savings, she was almost on the verge of suicide.

Despite herself, Susan is now listening

I did what I could, of course. Visited every few weeks and stayed a few days. Took her to London and Manchester. Saw some shows. But it was downhill all the way. That's why I asked her here. I thought the change would do her good. I had everything ready. Her favourite meal ... a bottle of wine ... tickets for the local amateurs — they were doing a Ray Cooney play, and I knew he was one of her favourites. But she never turned up. I couldn't understand it. It was so unlike her. I phoned the house for days, of course, but no one answered. That's why I finally called the police. I never dreamed she'd be up on the moor. I still can't believe it. (*She bursts into tears again*)

Diana (*putting her arm around Jessica's shoulders*) That's it. Have a good cry. I couldn't stop when my aunt vanished. She missed my graduation, and 's never been heard from since. A few years earlier and she could have been one of the ones buried up there.

Susan (*hotly*) No, she couldn't. She was nowhere near here when she vanished. She was on her way to Italy.

Diana I know. I'm just saying.

Susan (*acidly*) Well don't. (*She stands*) And I think we'd better go.

Jessica (*quickly*) No, please. I don't want to be alone. Let me make you that tea.

Diana Sue can do that, can't you, Sue?

Jessica (*rising*) No, no. It's all right. It gives me something to do.

She crosses to the kitchen and exits

The kitchen light goes on

Susan (*hissing in outrage*) Of all the thoughtless, insensitive people I've ever met ...

Diana (*protesting softly*) Oh, come on, Sue. She can't help it. She's upset.

Susan (*furiously*) It's you I'm talking about. I've never been so ashamed and embarrassed in my life. She's had the most horrible experience, and all you're interested in, is revelling in her misery.

Diana (*reasonably*) But it's something no one else has got, yet. An eye-witness account from the latest victim's friend. It could be the best bit in the book.

Susan (*seething*) Well as far as I'm concerned ...

There is a loud scream from the kitchen. They turn to the kitchen door, as Jessica stumbles out in a panic

Jessica (*terrified*) Someone outside. At the window. Looking in. And covered in blood. (*She sags*)

Susan supports Jessica. Diana hurries to the main door and begins to open it

Susan (*alarmed*) No, Diana. *No.*
Diana (*firmly*) Take care of her. I'll see to this. (*She opens the doors*)

Rhoda Bradstock stumbles into the porch. She is in her fifties, wearing mud-streaked dark slacks, a t-shirt, and mud-splattered walking shoes. Over this she wears a mud-streaked and dripping wet transparent plastic mac and hood. A nasty-looking gash is over one eye, and blood streams down her mud-streaked and wet face

Rhoda (*gasping*) Thank God you turned the light on. I hadn't a clue where I was. It's black as pitch out there and coming down in sheets. (*She introduces herself*) Rhoda Bradstock. I'm staying at the farmhouse. At least, I think I am. This is McBride's farm?
Diana (*stepping aside*) Yes. Yes. It is.
Rhoda (*entering gratefully*) Sorry about the fright. I didn't mean to startle you.

Susan and Jessica stare at her

Diana Your face. It's bleeding.
Rhoda (*touching her forehead and wincing*) I thought it must be. Saw enough stars to start a new galaxy.
Susan (*anxiously*) Has someone attacked you?
Rhoda (*amused*) No, no. It's my own stupid fault. I took the dog for a walk about an hour ago. Friendly old thing, isn't he? Follows me round like Mary's little lamb. Anyway, he seemed to know his way round without a lead, so we ended up on the moor near a pile of rocks a couple of miles away. Hardly had time to admire the view before the heavens opened, and he was off like a shot, tail between his legs.
Jessica (*shakily*) He's afraid of thunder.
Rhoda (*nodding*) That explains it, then. I thought I'd probably lost him.
Jessica (*shaking her head slightly*) He'll have made his way back here, as fast as he could. He's probably inside the barn.
Rhoda Anyway ... by the time I got my mac on ... lucky I was carrying it ... I could hardly see a thing. Five minutes later, I tripped over a root, or something, fell into a gully, and cracked my head on a boulder. God

knows where my specs went. Couldn't find them anywhere and can hardly see a thing without them. Been blundering round ever since, hoping I'd find the right track without breaking my neck ...

Jessica I'll get some warm water. For the cut.

Rhoda (*easily*) No, no. I'll be fine. Honestly, I will. Just a scratch, I expect.

Diana It looks deep to me. You might need stitches.

Susan (*helpfully*) Perhaps you should see a doctor?

Rhoda (*smiling*) I am a doctor.

They all look surprised

But not of medicine. Entomology's my field. The study of insects. That's why I'm booked in here. At the farm, I mean. Hoping for a few days of close encounters with all that's creepy and crawly. (*Wryly*) Providing anything's survived after that lot outside. (*She looks down*) Oh, God ... I'm dripping all over the carpet. (*Stepping back*) I'd better be off. But sorry about the fright. It wasn't intended. Truly, it wasn't.

There is another very loud crack of thunder

Jessica (*impulsively*) Why don't you stay a while? Until it eases off? I was just making tea. I'm sure you could do with a cup.

Rhoda Nothing I'd like better, but I've still got the key in my pocket. Don't want "mine host" coming back and finding she's locked out of her own house.

Jessica I shouldn't let that worry you. Donald's just left, and he's got his own set. You can have a cup of tea, then all walk over together. (*Lightly*) I can even loan you an umbrella.

Rhoda It's very tempting, but I really need a good soak and a change of clothes. Can't drive into Chellingford looking like this.

Diana Chellingford?

Rhoda For something to eat. There's a decent pub in the marketplace, according to Mrs McBride. Not too pricey, and good home cooking. Might as well give it a try.

Susan (*dismayed*) Do they not do meals here, then?

Diana (*rolling her eyes*) Not evening meals. I told you. Just bed and breakfast.

Susan (*protesting*) But that means driving in this.

Diana (*sarcastically*) We could always walk.

Rhoda I can give you a lift, if you'd like? No point taking two cars if we're going to the same place.

Diana and Susan look at each other

Jessica This is ridiculous. Why don't you all stay here and have dinner with me? It won't be anything exotic, but I'm not a bad cook. I've done the odd breakfasts when Millie's been ill, and I've pork chops and fish in the freezer. I could even do a spaghetti if you'd prefer? There's a bottle or two of Merlot in the cupboard.

Susan (*shaking her head*) It's very kind, but —

Diana (*firmly*) Sounds good to me. But we do insist on paying. Name your price and we have a deal.

Susan turns away in disbelief

Rhoda (*nonplussed*) I don't know what to say.

Jessica Just yes, will do. I know it sounds selfish, but I can't be on my own tonight.

Rhoda looks puzzled

I need someone here. At least till bedtime. Millie'll sleep over if I find I can't cope. So shall we say six thirty?

Rhoda (*giving in*) Six thirty it is, then. And thank you.

Rhoda exits into the porch, and after adjusting her hood, exits into the yard

Diana closes the doors

Jessica I'll make that tea.

Jessica exits into the kitchen again

Susan (*angrily*) That's the last straw, Diana. First thing tomorrow, I'm going home. You can do your precious book on your own.

Diana (*protesting*) But you can't go. How will I get back?

Susan You should have thought of that before you started exploiting Mrs ... (*She realizes she does not know the surname*) Jessica.

Diana (*surprised*) Exploiting?

Susan Yes. Exploiting. You can see how upset she is, but all you're interested in is getting inside information on the poor woman's friend.

Diana (*amazed*) And what's wrong with that? No one's going to be interested in a book full of stuff they already know. And besides ... the shock must be wearing off by now. She wouldn't offer to cook dinner for perfect strangers if she were on the edge of a nervous breakdown, would she?

Susan (*in disbelief*) I give up. I really do give up. (*She sits heavily in the arm chair*)

Diana (*sighing deeply*) All right. I'll tell you what we'll do.

Susan (*peevishly*) You needn't bother, because the answer's no.

Diana You don't know what I'm going to say, yet.

Susan And I don't want to. The answer's still no.

There is a knock at the door, and Mildred enters. She wears a scruffy raincoat, liberally spattered with rain and a wide-brimmed man's hat that is soaking wet. Soggy strands of hair emerge from beneath it. She carries a shopping bag, bulging with items

Mildred (*as she enters*) Bloody caravans. Another one off the road at Allen's Dip. Traffic's tailed back for —— (*She sees the two women*) Who are you?

Diana Diana Wishart and Susan Tonks. We're staying at the Farm.

Mildred (*tersely*) Then you've no right to be here. It's private, this is. Nothing to do with the Bed and Breakfast.

Jessica enters from the kitchen

Jessica (*as she enters*) It's all right, Millie. I asked them. I needed a bit of company.

Mildred (*grudgingly*) Well in that case, I suppose it's all right. But I'm here, now, so they can be getting along before it comes down again. It's just stopped, but it won't be for long. You mark my words.

Jessica I've just made some tea.

Diana (*brightly*) Can't let it go to waste.

Mildred glances at her balefully

Jessica (*to Mildred*) You'll have a cup with us? You look like you could use it.

Mildred I'd a coffee in Connell and Green's, but ... go on, then. I suppose I've got time. It's fish for tonight's meal, and I did the veg before I went out. There's enough for four, if you don't feel up to cooking your own, and you know you're always welcome.

Jessica I do. But I've invited all your guests for dinner. They couldn't drive to Chellingford in this. They don't know the road, like we do, and the Dip's a nightmare, even in good weather.

Diana Sue hates driving at night, and these narrow roads don't exactly help.

Jessica Anyway. Sit yourself down and I'll get another cup. (*She turns to exit into the kitchen*)

Mildred Oh. I saw the cupboard looked empty, this morning, so I brought you a few things back. (*She holds out the bag*) Coffee, sugar, jar of marmalade, etc. I'll send Gavin over with eggs. We can settle up, later.

Jessica Thank you.

Jessica takes the bag and exits into the kitchen

Mildred (*moving to the sofa*) So how did you find yourself round here? (*She unbuttons her coat and sits*) Farmhouse not comfortable enough?

Diana (*hastily*) No, no. I'm sure it's marvellous. It was a mix-up, actually. We arrived earlier than we'd anticipated, saw the notice, and thought we'd got the wrong place as everywhere was locked, and ...

Mildred (*sharply*) Locked?

Diana Mrs Brad ... bury had gone for a walk and didn't like leaving the door open.

Mildred (*tightly*) It's Bradstock. And she'd no right going out. She told me quite definitely, she'd keep an eye on things until I got back. I might have had customers.

Susan (*hastily*) She wasn't out long. We only just missed her. And Mrs ... Jessica ... told us we could wait here till you opened up again.

Mildred (*bluntly*) And you couldn't see she were in no condition to know what she were doing?

Diana Because of the shock, you mean? Well, yes. Of course we could. That's why we accepted. She was absolutely shaking. We couldn't have left her alone, the state she was in. It's not as if we didn't know what she was going through. It's happened to me, hasn't it, Sue?

Mildred What has?

Diana Shock. When Aunt Gerry disappeared, I nearly had a breakdown. It was months before I could pull myself together. I thought she'd been murdered.

Mildred And had she?

Diana (*taken aback*) Well, no. She'd simply thrown up her job and gone to Italy. I didn't know it then, of course ... none of us did ... till an email arrived at her office to say where she was and that she wouldn't be coming back. (*Ruefully*) We've not heard a word from her since, and it's been four years. I just hope she's happy.

Mildred (*relaxing*) Four years, you say? (*Oddly*) I lost my husband almost *ten* years ago. An accident in the top field. Tractor rolled on top of him and killed him outright.

Diana and Susan look sympathetic

(*Matter-of-factly*) Been drinking, according to the police. Never believed it, myself. He liked his drop of beer, but I never saw him the worse for it. Happier with a mug of tea than anything alcoholic, but according to the inquest, he should never have been driving.

Jessica enters from the kitchen, with a tray holding four cups and saucers, milk jug, teapot, sugar bowl and spoons

Jessica (*apologetically*) Here we are. Sorry it's taken so long, but I seemed to be on another planet. Everything happening in slow motion.

She hands the tray round and they take cups, helping themselves to milk and sugar, and sipping at random

Mildred (*sagely*) Told you that might happen. It's a funny thing, shock is. Takes folk different ways.
Jessica To tell you the truth, I think I'm over the worst. Now it's more anger. I can't imagine the mentality of whoever killed her. He must be insane.
Susan (*nodding*) How can anyone hate someone enough to kill them? Just because they're not perfect?
Jessica (*protesting*) But there was nothing wrong with Etta. She was as normal as I am. (*She puts the tray down on the dresser, takes her own cup and moves down R of the sofa*)
Diana (*thoughtfully*) Then maybe ... (*She stops*)

The others look at her

Maybe there's another reason?
Mildred (*balefully*) That took some working out.
Diana I mean ... maybe she saw something? Or heard something? Something she shouldn't have done? And had to be silenced.
Mildred (*dourly*) We're not in Agatha Christie land. Apart from Jessica, no one round here's ever set eyes on her before and she vanished thirty-odd miles away, not from Chellingford town centre. How could she have seen or heard something she wasn't supposed to?
Diana (*shrugging*) It was only a suggestion.

Susan (*reasonably*) And where she vanished from's got nothing to do with it, really. I mean ... two of the others came from London, didn't they? The ones they've identified. It said so on the news.

Jessica But they were ——

Diana (*cutting in*) Differently abled. (*She smiles sweetly at Susan*) Exactly. Which is why I think there's something strange about *this* murder.

Jessica and Mildred stare at her

Why would he stop killing women he thought imperfect, and start killing those who weren't? It doesn't make sense. In fact, it wouldn't surprise me to find out this murder's got nothing at all to do with the others.

Mildred (*acidly*) Then it's a good job nob'dies put you in charge. It's plain as the nose on your face. When you're dealing with them that's cracked, who knows what's going through their mind? So there was nothing wrong with Jessie's friend ... least nothing she knew about. But what was he seeing when he looked at her? Had she a spot on her cheek, or was her lipstick on crooked? Did she have false teeth, or have a wart on her chin? What was it he considered imperfect?

Jessica (*becoming upset again*) Nothing. There was nothing. She was just Etta.

Mildred Then why'd he beat her face to a pulp, the same as all the others?

Diana (*reasonably*) It could be a copycat murder. Lump it in with the rest of them, and let someone else take the blame.

Jessica bursts into tears again

Susan (*mortified*) Diana.

Diana (*defensively*) It has been known. (*To Jessica*) I'm sorry. I've got this awful habit of opening my mouth and putting both feet in it. The last thing I wanted to do was ——

Jessica (*struggling to control herself*) No, no. It's all right. Really, it is. I'm just being stupid. (*She mops her eyes with the back of her free hand*)

Mildred (*firmly*) No you're not, Jess. If there's one thing you're *definitely* not, it's stupid. You've every right to be upset. (*Disgustedly*) Us going on about it as though it's something on last night's television and nothing to do with real life. We should have had more sense. But that's it. It won't be mentioned again. You'll have enough on your plate when the police start calling round every few minutes. I had it all when Jack died. Couldn't get rid of them. It was bad enough losing him, but trying to deal with them, grieve, and keep the farm running, nearly finished me. Hadn't been for Donald, I don't know what I'd have done.

There is a hammering at the main door that startles them

Diana Shall I get it? (*She moves to the door and opens it*)

Gavin is standing at the door, wearing a shabby and wet mackintosh over his overalls

Gavin (*surprised at seeing her*) Lookin' for Mrs M. (*He peers past her*)
Mildred (*turning to see him, irritated*) What is it, now?

Diana moves to one side and Gavin enters

Gavin Seen the truck was back, so thought you might be round here.
Mildred Well I am. So what's the problem?
Gavin Need a hand in top field. Couple of sheep broke through, and old Boris won't stir himself till thunder's cleared.
Mildred (*impatiently*) Then get Donald to help you ... That's what I pay him for.
Gavin Thought of that. But haven't seen him for the last half hour. Looked all round the yard, I have.
Diana (*helpfully*) You'll probably find him at the farmhouse. He took our luggage up there a little while ago.
Gavin (*glancing at her*) Must be hiding himself, then. Gone right through it, I have. He's not in his room. Even tried the lavvy, but he weren't there, either. (*To Mildred*) And she aint seen him ... the new arrival ... 'cos I asked her. (*Turning back to Diana*) One of them wheely things, with handles, was it?
Diana (*thrown*) Sorry? (*Realizing*) Oh ... the case, you mean? Yes. Yes, it is. Why?
Gavin Sitting in the middle of the path, like Pithy on a rock. Nearly went ar —— (*he corrects himself*) head first over it. Didn't know who it belonged to, so I put it under the porch.
Susan (*surprised*) You mean he left it outside? In all that rain? (*She fumes*)
Mildred (*angrily*) He's not got the brains he was born with.
Gavin (*sulkily*) Been acting strange, most the afternoon. Nearly bit my head off when I asked him what was wrong. Said it was all lies.
Mildred What was?

Gavin How should I know? Hardly talks to me, the best of times. But he did say he'd a call to make, and the minute you got back, there was going to be fireworks.

Mildred (*grimly*) Well he's not wrong, there. I don't know what bee he's got in his bonnet, but the sooner he gets rid of it, the better. (*She rises*) Thanks for the tea, Jess. (*She hands her the cup*) I'll sort this out, whatever it is, and see you later.

There is a flash of lightning, followed by a loud crack of thunder

Diana Looks like the fireworks have started.

Mildred and Gavin move towards the open door

As they do so, Adrian dashes into the porch and appears in the doorway. He wears a dripping wet plastic mackintosh over a light sweater, summer jacket and dark trousers

Adrian (*panting*) Talk about rain. It's like a monsoon, out there. (*He shakes his mackintosh*)

Jessica (*surprised*) Mr Brookes.

Adrian (*breathing heavily*) Sorry I couldn't make it sooner. They're still moving wreckage in Allen's Dip. But I came as soon as I got your message.

Jessica looks at him blankly

You wanted to see me.

Jessica (*blankly*) No.

Adrian (*puzzled*) But you told the manager. At the hotel. You said you'd remembered something.

Jessica No.

Adrian About my sister.

Jessica I'm sorry. I don't know what you're talking about.

Adrian (*protesting*) But he wrote it down. (*He fumbles in his pocket*) I've got it here. (*He produces the message. Reading*) "Adrian Brookes. Must see you. I remember something about your sister. Could be important. Jessica Scanlon." (*He looks up*)

Jessica (*puzzled*) But that's ridiculous. I never sent that.

Adrian (*baffled*) Then who did? It's got your name, and everything.

Jessica I couldn't possibly have sent it. To begin with, I'd no idea where you were staying. You never told me.

Adrian (*realizing*) That's right. (*He looks at Mildred and Gavin*) The only ones I did mention it to ... were Mrs McBride and him.

Mildred (*bridling*) Well it's no use looking at me. I've been out all afternoon and wouldn't have had time for practical jokes, even if I'd approved of them. Which I don't.

Diana (*chipping in*) Was it a woman who left the message? Or could it have been a man?

Adrian (*blankly*) I haven't a clue. They just gave it to me when I got back. I'd been over to Selwick to see if anyone there had seen Laura. It could have been anybody, I suppose. (*Firmly*) But I'm going to find out.

Gavin (*suddenly*) Don Caffrey made a call.

They all look at him

(*Awkwardly*) I told you. Did it about an hour ago.

Mildred (*sharply*) And why would *he* send fake messages?

Gavin (*muttering*) Told you he was acting funny.

Mildred And how would he know where to send it even if he —— (*She suddenly stops*)

Jessica (*frowning*) Millie?

Mildred (*remembering*) *I* told him, didn't I? Said I'd sooner be found dead in a ditch than lodge at *The Wild Goose*. (*Dismissively*) But he'd not do a thing like that. Not even as a joke. I've known him forty years or more. There's not a nasty bone in his body.

Adrian All the same, I'd like to have a word with him. If he did send this, I want to know what the hell he's playing at. And if he can't come up with a good answer ...

Mildred I'll go seek him out. He can't be far off.

Mildred exits, followed by Gavin

Diana closes the door

Adrian (*awkwardly*) I'm sorry about this. I really thought you had sent it. I mean ... who else knew why I was here ... in this neck of the woods? If you had remembered something ... even the briefest glimpse of her ... it'd be a step in the right direction. And after this morning ... (*He stops*)

Jessica (*to Diana and Susan*) He's looking for his sister. Another one who's suddenly gone missing. (*She sits heavily on the sofa*)

Diana (*interest flaring*) On the Moor, do you think?

Susan (*snapping*) Diana.

Adrian (*helplessly*) It's where she was seen last. At least I think it is. (*He sighs deeply*) To tell you the truth, I'm starting to wonder if I'm not just clutching at straws. Every time I see someone who looks like her from the back, my heart skips a beat ... but the minute they turn round ... the resemblance is gone. She could be anywhere by this time.

Diana (*moving down* L) I know how you feel. When my aunt vanished, I saw her everywhere. In town, the supermarkets, the clubs ... anywhere but Italy.

Adrian Italy?

Diana That's where she'd gone. She sent us an email. (*Flippantly*) Not coming back. Stuff the job and you can tell the mayor what he can do with his little cocked hat and chain. Never heard from her since.

Adrian (*staring at her*) But that's ... terrible.

Diana Not if you knew the mayor. Pompous old pratt, he was. But Italy was the mystery. She didn't know a word of the language and couldn't eat the food. Allergic to wheat and things, so she couldn't pig out on sphagetti bol like the rest of us. No. If she'd said Greece or Turkey, we could have understood it, but *Italy* ...

Jessica (*looking up*) Would — would you mind moving back to the farmhouse? Just until dinner. I can't take everything in. I don't know what's happening.

Diana (*contrite*) Oh, my God. Of course. Here we are babbling on and ... (*To Susan*) Come on, Sue. I *said* we should give her some peace and quiet.

Susan gapes at her

(*To Jessica*) She never did know how to take a hint. We'll make a dash for it now and see you in a couple of hours. Mr Brookes can hide us under his mac.

The door bursts open and Mildred staggers into the room

Mildred (*gasping*) It's Donald. He's hanged himself. Inside the barn.

They all stare at her as the scene ends

ACT II

Scene 1

Two hours later

The tea things have been cleared away, the curtains are now open again, and outside looks quite gloomy. Otherwise the room is as before and the main door is closed. Jessica sits on the sofa looking exhausted and Detective Inspector Tyson sits in the easy chair, facing her. He/she is in his/her forties, appears kindly and sympathetic, but is endowed with a ruthless determination to get to the bottom of things. He/she wears informal clothing. Detective Sergeant Morley is standing by the kitchen door, taking notes. He/she is in his/her thirties, and wears a suit

Tyson And that was the last you saw of him? When he took the suitcase and left?

Jessica (*dully*) Yes.

Tyson And he was heading for the farmhouse?

Jessica (*nodding tiredly*) Yes.

Tyson But we now know, he never got there. Just left the case in the middle of the path, went into the barn and hanged himself. Why do you think he did that?

Jessica does not reply

Mrs Scanlon?

Jessica looks at him/her blankly

Have you any idea why he did that?

Jessica (*shaking her head*) No.

Tyson (*pressing*) None at all?

Jessica (*irritably*) Of course not. Why would I?

Tyson (*mildly*) Could it be something to do with the discovery of your friend's body this morning?

Jessica (*taken aback*) What on earth gave you that idea?

Tyson (*shrugging*) He was supposed to pick her up from the station, if I understand rightly?

Jessica But she never turned up. I told you that last week.

Tyson Actually, you told me he *said* she hadn't turned up.

Jessica And she didn't. That's why Gavin went to town to meet the next train. To see if she was on that.

Tyson That's Gavin ... (*he thinks*) ... Purdie? Mrs McBride's other farmhand?

Jessica Yes.

Tyson So why didn't Mr Caffrey wait for the next train?

Jessica (*irritated*) I don't know. I can't remember. There was something wrong with the tractor, I think, and Donald's the one who dealt with the farm vehicles. Gavin only drives when the others are busy.

Tyson But Donald was the first to know that Mrs Lipton wasn't on the train?

Jessica (*impatiently*) Yes. He called from the station. I've already said.

Tyson And how did you know where he was when he called?

Jessica Because he told me. He was at the station, and she hadn't got off the train.

Tyson (*leaning forwards*) But what if she had been on the train, Mrs Scanlon? What then? (*He/she resumes his original position*)

Jessica (*blankly*) I'm sorry?

Tyson Isn't it possible she was collected by Mr Caffrey, then taken on to the moor and murdered before he telephoned to say she hadn't arrived?

Jessica (*in disbelief*) It's totally impossible. What are you saying? That Donald was lying?

Tyson (*mildly*) There is that possibility. One of the advantages of modern technology ... at least from a criminal's point of view ... is the fact that when using a mobile phone, the person on the other end has no idea if you're really where you say you are. You could tell them you were in China, but actually be in the next room.

Jessica (*tartly*) The question wouldn't arise in Donald's case. He didn't have a mobile phone. I doubt he could have used one if his life depended on it. He called from the station phone. I could hear the train in the background.

Tyson (*after a moment*) You hadn't mentioned that.

Jessica Why should I? Do you question everything people tell you? (*She remembers*) Yes. I suppose you do. Part of your job, I expect. (*Firmly*) But I knew Donald Caffrey for four years, and he was the kindest, most honest man I've ever met. The suggestion that he could have killed Etta's the most ridiculous thing I've ever heard.

Tyson (*after staring at her for a moment*) So you'd rule him out, completely?

Jessica (*firmly*) Yes. I would.

Tyson (*after a slight pause*) Have you any idea how long he'd been employed here, Mrs Scanlon?

Jessica (*unsure*) About ten years, I think. You'd have to ask Millie ... Mrs McBride. It was just after Jack ... her husband ... died. She couldn't cope with only Gavin to help. Why do you ask?

Tyson The bodies on the moor. They've been there for some time. Twenty years, in some cases.

Jessica (*horrified*) You're not suggesting ——

Tyson (*cutting in*) Anything, Mrs Scanlon. (*Lightly*) Until we've more evidence, I'm simply theorizing. Examining possibilities.

Jessica (*firmly*) Well that's one possibility you can forget, Inspector Tyson. Donald Caffrey had nothing to do with Etta Lipton's murder, or anyone else's for that matter. He didn't know she existed till last week.

Tyson It's nice to know he has such a staunch defender, Mrs Scanlon. (*Rising*) Well thank you for your time. I expect we'll meet again.

DI Morley closes his/her notepad

Jessica (*frowning*) Why should we? I've told you all I know.

Tyson (*smiling*) There's always something slips the memory. Bit like a jigsaw puzzle, actually. The full picture only emerges when all the pieces are in the right place.

Tyson frowns and extracts a mobile phone from his/her pocket and replies

Yes? (*A pause*) Does it, indeed? (*A pause*) Yes. Yes. Well spotted. I'll be there in half a minute.

He/she ends the call, replaces the phone and indicates for Morley to go

Morley opens the main door and exits R

(*To Jessica*) I'd have a word with your doctor, if I were you. You might need something to settle you. Two bodies in one day's enough for anyone. Even me.

Tyson follows Morley out, closing the door behind him/her

Jessica closes her eyes and retreats into a world of her own. After a moment, there is a gentle knock on the door, but she fails to respond

A moment later, it cautiously opens and Diana sidles round the edge of it

Diana (*seeing Jessica and hissing*) Jessica? (*She closes the door swiftly*)

There is still no response

(*Moving to Jessica's side*) Are you all right?

There is still no reaction, so Diana shakes her gently

Jessica (*snapping out of her reverie*) Hmm?
Diana (*accusingly*) They didn't bully you, did they?
Jessica Of course not. Why should they?
Diana (*perching on the sofa arm*) Well what did they want with you? I told them we were here when he did it, and we didn't know a thing till Mrs McBride came back, so there wasn't any point.

Jessica closes her eyes and turns her head away

(*Indignantly*) Honestly. Anybody'd think we'd put the rope round his neck, the way they were going on. They even criticized Adrian for cutting him down. (*Scornfully*) He shouldn't have touched him, they said. He'd interfered with the evidence. (*Indignantly*) "He could still have been alive," I told the snotty one, "And Sue's in the St John's Ambulance, so she knows all there is to know about artificial respiration. She'd have had him breathing in no time if his neck hadn't been broken." I mean ... he'd not been dangling that long, had he? He was still warm. (*Concerned*) Are you sure they didn't bully you? You're awfully pale.
Jessica (*distractedly*) What are you doing here?
Diana (*concerned*) Worrying about you. You've had one nasty shock today, and the last thing you needed was something like this happening. I said they hadn't to bother you, but they insisted on interviewing everybody ... (*Rolling her eyes*) "To get a clearer picture". (*Snorting*) Well I didn't like their attitude, so as soon as they left the farmhouse, I followed them round here and hid outside to keep an eye on things. (*Firmly*) They weren't browbeating you if *I'd* anything to do with it. One wrong word, and I'd have been in here like a shot. (*She remembers*) Did they ask you about the suicide note?
Jessica (*surprised*) What suicide note?
Diana (*nodding*) Exactly. "I thought you were detectives," I said. "How many people have you come across who write suicide notes in pouring rain before topping themselves?" (*Frowning*) It is odd though, isn't it? I mean ... he was fine a few minutes earlier. Not depressed, or anything. So why would he want to kill himself? (*She looks at Jessica again*) Are you sure you're all right? I'll make some tea, shall I?

Jessica (*attempting to be polite*) No thank you. I think I'd rather have some time alone.

Diana (*sympathetically*) Of course, you would. You look awful. I don't know how you're coping. Anyone else would be screaming for tranquillizers. (*Indignantly*) You'd think they'd have more sense than to start asking questions after the kind of day you've had. (*Scornfully*) But that's the police, all over. Not a scrap of sensitivity when it comes to people's feelings. (*She rises*) I'll get back to the farmhouse, then. I think Mrs M could do with a bit of cheering up. (*She moves to the door, then turns back*) Oh ... and we're still on for half past, aren't we? Or would you like to put it back a bit?

Jessica looks at her, blankly

(*Prompting*) The dinner.

Jessica (*remembering*) Dinner? Oh, no. (*She rises, looking distressed*) I'm so sorry. I don't think I can. (*Helplessly*) I mean ... with Donald's suicide and the police questioning ... I just ... can't. Even the *thought* of cooking ... (*She stops*)

Diana (*dismayed*) But we've not eaten since —— (*Recovering*) Well. It's not a problem, is it? We can drive into Chellingford, and have a meal there, I suppose. (*With mock concern*) But what about you? Shall we bring something back?

Jessica (*shaking her head*) I couldn't eat a thing. Honestly.

Diana (*grimacing*) Mrs M's not feeling good, either. Decidedly on the shaky side.

Jessica I'm not surprised. They'd known each other for years. (*Almost to herself*) I just can't think why he did it.

Diana (*surprised*) Didn't they tell you? They were dropping hints like bricks when they questioned us. (*Gleefully*) They think he was responsible for the bodies on the moor, and committed suicide when he thought they were on his track.

Jessica Which is absolutely ridiculous. He wouldn't have hurt a fly.

Diana (*back-tracking*) Exactly my own opinion. If you ask me, they haven't a clue who killed them. They're just trying to make themselves look good because they're not getting anywhere, and who better to blame than some poor devil who's no longer here to defend himself.

There is a knock on the door

Jessica (*calling weakly*) Come in.

The door opens and Susan enters. She wears a rain hood and jacket with a sprinkle of rain-drops on them. She sees Diana

Susan (*icily*) Oh. I didn't know *you* were round here. I came to see Mrs Scanlon. (*To Jessica*) I'm sorry to bother you, but Mrs McBride's really upset, and I can't see her cooking tonight, so would you mind awfully if Gavin came over as well? He hasn't a clue how to cook for himself.

Diana (*rolling her eyes again*) For heaven's sake. He can make a *sandwich*, can't he? Anyway ... there's been a change of plan. Jessica's not feeling up to it, either, so we'll have to get Rhoda to run us into town and we'll eat there.

Jessica (*apologetically*) I'm so sorry.

Susan (*hastily*) No, no. I said we shouldn't be imposing on you. I've been feeling guilty ever since we accepted. (*Brightly*) And we'd have had to eat out, anyway, if this hadn't happened. (*Wryly*) Not that anyone's particularly hungry, now.

Diana (*incredulously*) Speak for yourself. *I* could eat a horse.

Susan (*ignoring this*) And it would solve the problem, wouldn't it? We could take Gavin with us.

Diana (*protesting*) Hang on a minute. We hardly know him. (*To Jessica*) He is all right, isn't he? You know? Not a few sandwiches short of a picnic?

Susan (*mortified*) Diana.

Diana (*ignoring her*) I mean ... he does seem a bit peculiar.

Jessica (*nonplussed*) I can't say I'd noticed.

Diana Well he doesn't say much, does he? Just creeps around, looking at you from the corner of his eye. He's been like a cat on hot bricks since the police arrived. Twitching and jumping every time they looked in his direction. And he could hardly hold his tea. Half of it slopped down his shirt. (*Distastefully*) Not that he noticed. It just added to last month's dinners.

Susan (*firmly*) Well I thought it looked like shock. I mean ... they'd worked together for years, hadn't they? So it'd only be natural after seeing him like that. But he said he was fine when I asked him. And I did put extra sugar in his mug, which must have helped, because he seemed a lot better after they'd finished asking questions.

Diana (*sourly*) I still don't see why we should be lumbered with him. He's not my idea of an ideal dinner companion.

Susan (*tartly*) And at this precise moment, Diana, having dinner with you isn't mine. But if we're going to ask Rhoda to drive us into Chellingford, we'd better get a move on. It's after six now and I'd like to get there before the rain starts again. (*To Jessica*) It's been lovely meeting you, Mrs Scanlon. I just wish it had been in happier circumstances.

Diana (*amused*) We're not leaving the country, Sue. We can pop round anytime for the next few days. Maybe have tea together? (*She looks at Jessica for confirmation*)

Susan (*smiling tightly*) Rather a long trip, wouldn't you say? For me, at
least. Close on eighty miles, the last time I checked.

Diana (*puzzled*) Eighty miles? (*She realizes*) Oh, come on, Sue. You're
not serious? You're not really going?

Susan (*firmly*) I am. I told you I was. I'll leave you the car, but first
thing in the morning, I'll be catching the train home.

Diana (*sourly*) And wanting me to take you to the station, I expect?

Susan Not at all. I can walk it from the hotel. It's only five minutes
away.

Diana (*taken aback*) What hotel?

Susan I've booked a room at the *Grapes and Pheasant*.

Diana looks at her in surprise

Well I'm certainly not sleeping here, am I? Not after what's happened.
I couldn't close my eyes. The minute dinner was over, I was leaving.
(*Seething*) And the only reason I was staying for that, was because
Mrs Scanlon kindly offered to feed us ... perfect strangers ... in spite
of being in no condition to do so ... and I was going to make quite sure
you didn't spend all evening trying to con her into telling you her life
story so you could use it in your rotten book.

Jessica Book? (*She looks at Diana*)

Susan (*acidly*) Didn't she tell you why we came here? She's planning
on writing a book about the Moor Murders, and can't wait to add your
friend's name to the roll call of victims. And now the police think
Mr Caffrey murdered them, she's in seventh heaven. (*Scornfully*)
I'm sure she'll have a whole new chapter in mind now. (*She quotes*)
"My terrifying meeting with Britain's most deranged serial killer."
(*Bitterly*) Well I want nothing to do with it. Nothing at all.

Susan turns and exits rapidly, almost in tears

Jessica looks at Diana in stony silence

Diana (*attempting to laugh it off*) With friends like Sue, who on earth
needs enemies? (*Lightly*) She's my best friend, but I've never known
anyone like her for getting things wrong. I am planning a book, yes.
And it is about the murders on Chellingford Moor ... but where she got
the idea I intended including your friend in it, I can't imagine. I mean
... they're obviously not connected, are they? The others were killed
years ago, according to the police. Twenty, in some cases. It can't
possibly be the same killer.

Jessica (*shakily*) I think you'd better go.

Diana (*hastily*) I wouldn't dream of writing anything that might offend you ... especially after today. If you'll listen for a minute ——
Jessica (*cutting in*) I really don't want to know. Now if you wouldn't mind.
Diana It's just a misunderstanding. I can promise you ——

Inspector Tyson appears behind Diana

Tyson (*cordially*) Miss Wishart?

Diana turns, startled

Diana (*flustered*) Inspector Tyson. I was just leaving.
Tyson (*smiling*) In that case, I won't delay you. (*He/she enters the room and steps aside*)

Diana exits rapidly, closing the door behind her

(*To Jessica*) Sorry to bother you again. But there's something I forgot to ask.
Jessica (*apprehensively*) Oh?
Tyson (*easily*) It's nothing important. Just something that's been niggling at me since last week.
Jessica Yes?
Tyson Why didn't *you* collect your friend from the station?
Jessica (*thrown*) I ... I don't drive.
Tyson Ah.
Jessica And even if I did, it made sense for Donald to meet her, because of him being in town that morning. Collecting feed and things.
Tyson In the lorry outside the small barn?
Jessica Yes. And please don't look so disapproving, Inspector. There was nothing snobbish about Etta. She was a country girl, like me, and being met by a farm lorry wouldn't have worried her in the least. Besides, it gave me time to prepare the meal and tidy up the guest room. I use it as a studio if I'm here on my own ... which is usually the case.
Tyson How often did she visit here, Mrs Scanlon?
Jessica She didn't. I told you that last week. It would have been her first time ... which is why your suggestion that Donald could have killed her is so ridiculous.
Tyson But you visited her? In Tamstock.
Jessica Of course. Whenever she seemed to need me.
Tyson And how often was that, if you don't mind my asking?

Jessica (*blankly*) I've no idea. Every few weeks, I suppose. Whenever she got depressed.

Tyson Depressed?

Jessica (*annoyed*) Her husband was killed in a car crash and she was struggling to adjust without him. I told you this in my statement. Doesn't anybody read them? (*She sighs deeply*) Sometimes she was so distraught, she'd take off for days on end.

Tyson And where did she go?

Jessica (*shrugging*) I've no idea. (*Trying to remember*) There was an hotel in Harrogate, once. And a rest home somewhere near Scarborough. But she rarely told anyone where she'd been or what she'd done.

Tyson (*drily*) Not even her best friend?

Jessica (*quietly*) She was a very private person.

Tyson So it would seem. And what about Mr Caffrey? Did he take time off from his farm work?

Jessica (*frowning*) You'd have to ask Millie, that. But it's very unlikely. Working a farm ... even as small as this one ... with only two helpers, doesn't leave much time for days off. Even I've helped out at harvest time. But as far as I remember, he'd not spent a night away in the last four years.

Tyson (*giving a frustrated sigh*) Pity. If I could only prove that he and Mrs Lipton had met before, I could wrap this case up in the next twenty-four hours.

Jessica And I keep telling you you're making a mistake. Why won't you listen?

Tyson (*firmly*) Because the evidence we found near Mrs Lipton's body seems pretty conclusive. Whoever dumped her body there, had to have transport, and luckily for us, because there's been no rain for the past fortnight, we found a tyre print of the vehicle that most probably did the job. A print that appears to match the tyres on Mr Caffrey's lorry.

Jessica (*shaken*) I don't believe it.

Tyson (*lightly*) We'll have to take a closer look, of course. Get forensics to check the cabin for DNA, etcetera. If she was inside it, there's a good chance we'll find something.

Jessica And if there isn't?

Tyson (*shrugging*) Then we're back to square one. (*He/she prepares to exit*) But I'm sure that won't happen, Mrs Scanlon. (*Drily*) We may not be as well equipped as our television counterparts in the USA, but our forensic team are still rather good. I'm sure we'll not be disappointed.

Tyson opens the door and exits, closing it behind him/her

Jessica gazes at the closed door as though in a trance. After a moment, she moves blindly to the sofa and sits, mind working furiously

A moment later, she stands again and unsteadily crossing to the kitchen, exits

There is a knock on the door and it opens to reveal Gavin, who has cleaned himself up and slicked his hair. He wears a grubby-looking shirt and tie, and a dark suit, obviously made for a somewhat larger person. He carries a small wicker basket, covered with a cloth

Gavin (*glancing around*) You there, Jessie?

There is no reply

Brought you some eggs from Mrs M. Reckoned you hadn't got none.

Jessica enters from the kitchen, carrying a glass of orange juice

Jessica (*halting, startled*) Gavin. I didn't hear you.
Gavin (*displaying the basket*) Eggs. Mrs told me you needed 'em.
Jessica (*putting the glass on the mantlepiece*) You needn't have bothered tonight. There was no hurry. (*She takes the basket*) How's she feeling?
Gavin Be better when that lot have gone. Not seen her like this since Jack died. Tough as old boots, usually. Knowed Caffrey forty years or more, she did. S'posed to be getting wed next Spring, they was.
Jessica (*surprised*) Millie and Donald?
Gavin (*nodding*) Heard her telling the foreign tart, couple of weeks ago. (*Scornfully*) Going to Paris for their honeymoon, she said. (*He snorts*) What they want with honeymoons at their time of life? And who'd look after the place while they were gone, eh? 'Spect they'd have wanted me. (*Sourly*) Wouldn't be nobody else, I can tell you.
Jessica (*kindly*) They'd have known it was in safe hands, Gavin. (*She frowns*) But why didn't they tell me?
Gavin (*sourly*) Didn't tell me, neither. Hadn't been for the door being half open, I'd never have known. (*Anxiously*) But don't you let on I told you.
Jessica Of course not. (*Curiously*) But who's the foreign tar —— woman?
Gavin (*scornfully*) Stayed here while you was gone to your friend's. Stuck-up piece wi' a funny accent who thought she were too grand to mix wi' common farmhands. (*Smirking*) Didn't stop her choking, though, did it?
Jessica (*surprised*) Choking?

Gavin Dozen times a day, 'cording to Mrs. Went a funny colour and had to use one of them little blowy things to get her breath back.

Jessica (*realizing*) She had asthma.

Gavin Reckoned old Boris were setting her off. Or mebbe the cats. Didn't stay long, in any case. Slung her hook after a couple of days. Good riddance to bad rubbish, to my way of thinking. Anyway ... can't stand here talking. Eating in town wi' the ladies and don't want to keep 'em waiting. (*Uncertainly*) Y' reckon I look decent enough? Not used to dressing up smart, and things.

Jessica (*tactfully*) You look very well turned out.

Gavin (*looking at himself*) One of Jack's old suits. Mrs gave 'em to me. And his shirts and things. Got my own boots, though. Feet's too small for his. (*Ruefully*) Wouldn't have minded his Sunday best. Hand-made'ns, they was. Allus wore 'em for church.

Jessica (*smiling wanly*) It's a long time since *I* went there.

Gavin Not been myself since he died. None of us have. Daren't miss, before the accident, but we'd had enough hell and damnation to last a lifetime, by the day they buried him. (*Sourly*) Should have been a preacher, 'stead of running a farm. Did him no good, though, all his ranting an' raving. Reckon losing the kiddie turned him to drink. Could hardly walk the night he took tractor on top field. No wonder he tipped it over. Bad enough slope when you've got your wits about you, but having a bottle of whiskey inside you ...

Rhoda and Susan appear behind him. Rhoda wears a summer raincoat over a light dress, and has a plaster on her forehead. Susan has also changed into a skirt, blouse and summer jacket

Rhoda (*uncertainly*) Are you ready, Mr Purdie?

Susan (*disapprovingly*) We've been waiting in the yard.

Gavin moves hastily aside as Rhoda and Susan enter

Jessica (*apologetically*) It's my fault, I'm afraid. He came over with eggs (*she shows the basket*) and I kept him talking. I'm so sorry.

Rhoda (*hastily*) It's no problem. We're not in a hurry. But the police have gone now and the rain's stopped, so I'd like to be away before it starts up again. The forecast's pretty dreadful. (*She hesitates*) Are you sure you won't come with us, Mrs Scanlon? There's plenty of room, now Diana's decided to give it a miss.

Jessica (*surprised*) She's not going?

Susan (*drily*) Suddenly lost her appetite.

Rhoda But she's promised to keep an eye on Mrs McBride, which I think is a good idea. She really ought to be seeing a doctor. You both should. I can't believe they didn't insist on it.

Gavin Not seen a doctor in thirty years, Mrs hasn't. Got no time for 'em, she says. More faith in Arthur Collins.

Rhoda glances at him questioningly

Jessica (*explaining*) The local vet.

Rhoda (*to Jessica*) I hadn't realized when you offered to cook for us. No one had said anything, and I wouldn't have dreamed of ——

Jessica (*quickly*) No, no. It's all right. Really it is. I'm fine. I just need a little time alone and a good night's sleep. I'm sure I'll feel better in the morning. (*She forces a smile*) Drive carefully.

Rhoda, Susan and Gavin turn to leave

(*Suddenly*) Did you find another pair?

Rhoda turns back, puzzled

Susan and Gavin exit into the porch

(*Prompting*) Of spectacles.

Rhoda (*blankly*) Spectacles? (*Remembering*) Oh, no. No. I must have left them at home. (*She smiles*) Good job I'm not dependent. I should be able to drive all right if I take it slowly. With a bit of luck, I can pick up a temporary pair tomorrow, or retrace my steps and find the ones I lost. I've a rough idea where I missed my footing, and the daylight'll help.

Jessica stares at her

(*Uncertainly*) Well ... Good-night, then.

Rhoda exits, closing the door behind them

Jessica remains unmoving, then glances down at the egg basket she is holding. For a moment she appears not to recognize what it is

Then she slowly exits into the kitchen again

A few moments later, she re-emerges, still looking dazed, absently picks up the glass of orange juice, moves distractedly to the sofa and sits

Suddenly she burst into tears again, then pulls herself together and takes a gulp of the juice

Adrian passes the window without her noticing

Rising, Jessica heads for the stairs with a determined look on her face. As she is about to exit, Adrian knocks on the door, startling her

Jessica (*uncertainly*) Who is it?
Adrian (*off*) Adrian. Adrian Brookes.

Jessica puts the glass on the dresser and crosses to the door

Jessica What do you want?
Adrian (*off*) It's urgent. I need to talk to you.
Jessica What about?
Adrian (*off*) It'd be better without the door between us.
Jessica (*after a moment*) Give me a moment. (*She mops at her eyes and tidies her hair before taking a breath and opening the door*)

Adrian stands there, minus the plastic mac

Adrian Thank you. (*He enters the room*)

Jessica closes the door

I've been sitting in the car for the last half hour. Wondering what to do. (*He stops*)
Jessica (*after a moment*) About what?
Adrian (*awkwardly*) Do you mind if we sit? You still seem a bit unsteady.

Jessica stares at him a moment, then indicates the arm chair. He moves to it and sits. She sits on the sofa

(*Reluctantly*) I've not been entirely honest with you. About who I am.
Jessica Oh?
Adrian (*hastily*) There's nothing to worry about. I'm exactly who I said I was. I just didn't trot out the full title. (*He gives a weak smile*) I'm actually *Detective Sergeant* Brookes. South Yorkshire police. I'd show you my warrant, but I must have left it in my suit.
Jessica (*puzzled*) Then ...?

Adrian What am I doing here? Exactly what I said I was doing. Looking for my sister. But it seems I've been wasting my time.

Jessica You've heard from her?

Adrian (*shaking his head*) She's still missing. But according to DI Tyson, two days after the appeal went out, a student from Redcar came forward. She'd been camping on the moor, doing research. Pure coincidence she'd a similar naevus, so I'm back where I started. But that's not what I came to see you about. (*He takes a deep breath*) Are you quite sure that Donald Caffrey didn't kill Etta Lipton?

Jessica (*firmly*) Of course I'm sure. I told Inspe ——

Adrian (*cutting in*) Then if he didn't do it, is there any chance that Gavin Purdie could have?

Jessica (*startled*) Gavin? (*Recovering*) Well, of course he couldn't. Why are you saying that?

Adrian Because it seems he's drawn police attention at various times in the past. Two accusations of sexual assault on teenage girls and one of indecent exposure. Nothing was ever proved ... the McBrides gave him perfect alibis ... but all the same ...

Jessica (*shocked*) You're wrong. You must be wrong.

Adrian (*shaking his head*) It's all on record. And there's something else. The message I got at *The Wild Goose*. That you wanted to see me. I checked with the landlord. It was definitely a man who left it. And if it wasn't Donald Caffrey, it had to be Gavin Purdie.

Jessica (*protesting*) No, it didn't. It could have been anyone.

Adrian (*shaking his head*) They were the only two men who knew I'd been here to see you, who I was looking for, and where I was staying. What I can't work out, is why he did it. It doesn't make sense. Why did he want me back here?

Jessica (*firmly*) You don't know that he did. And if you're so suspicious of Gavin, why are you telling me all this? You should be telling Inspector Tyson.

Adrian (*ruefully*) I already have. But she/he's so convinced that Caffrey did the moor killings, she/he won't even consider an alternative theory. That's why I need *your* help.

Jessica (*surprised*) Mine?

Adrian To find the real murderer. (*He rises and paces the room*) I just know Don Caffrey had nothing to do with these killings. I met the man and liked him. No way am I going to stand by and let an innocent man take the rap for something he hasn't done.

Jessica (*puzzled*) But what can I do?

Adrian Can you take your mind back to the day Mrs Lipton was due to arrive? What happened when she failed to turn up? Did he come back here?

Jessica Well ... yes. There were two and a half hours before the next
train arrived, and Millie was waiting for the supplies he'd gone for.

Adrian And it's a fifteen minute drive, or thereabouts?

Jessica I suppose so. Yes.

Adrian So how long did he wait at the station when he found out she
wasn't on the train?

Jessica (*blankly*) Just long enough to call Millie and pass on the
message. There's no phone in the cottage, and I don't have a mobile.
(*Embarrassed*) I'm a bit like Donald. I like my solitude.

Adrian So assuming five minutes, plus the drive back, he'd be here
twenty minutes after the train had arrived?

Jessica nods

(*Triumphantly*) Which means he couldn't possibly have taken her on
to the moor, killed her, hidden the body then driven back here. There
wasn't the time. I knew it.

Jessica But you've still not explained how *I* can help.

Adrian (*firmly*) I need someone to keep an eye on Purdie. If I'm right,
he's as mad as a hatter. God knows how many he's actually killed.
There could be another dozen or so up there, just waiting for someone
to find them. But I won't be around for the next few days. I'm due
back at work on Monday, and have to leave tomorrow. The thing is,
now he thinks Caffrey's going to take the blame, he's bound to drop
his guard and do something stupid. (*Grimly*) And that's when we'll
have him.

Jessica And what about Donald?

Adrian As soon as we can prove Purdie's the real killer, Tyson'll have
to admit they've made a mistake.

Jessica (*quietly*) But it won't bring him back, will it?

Adrian (*ruefully*) No.

Jessica If only we knew why he killed himself.

Adrian (*hesitating*) I'm not so sure that he did.

Jessica stares at him

Obviously I'm not an expert, but I've seen enough suicides to know
there was something strange about the whole scenario. I noticed it
when I cut him down. There were no scratch marks round his neck ...
where he'd tried to loosen the rope. Even the most determined suicide
does it ... it's an instinctive reaction to choking. If I had to take a guess,
I'd say he was dead before the rope went round his neck.

Jessica (*horrified*) Oh, my God.

Adrian But if that's what really happened, it won't be long before the evidence proves it. They'll probably do a post mortem tomorrow. But in the meantime ——

There is a banging on the door, and it opens to reveal a distraught and coatless Mildred who staggers into the room

Mildred Donald. They're blaming Donald. They're saying he killed them all.

Adrian (*quickly*) It's all right. They'll never be able to prove it.

Mildred (*wildly*) We've got to help him. Tell them the truth. He didn't do it.

Jessica (*rising and hurrying to her*) Of course he didn't. We know that, Millie. (*She puts her arm around her*) And we're going to prove they're wrong. (*She leads Millie to the sofa*)

Mildred (*sobbing*) It wasn't him. He'd nothing to do with it. It was my fault. Mine.

Diana appears in the doorway. She too is coatless

Diana (*gasping breathlessly*) I thought she was still in her room. I couldn't stop her. (*She enters*)

Mildred (*collapsing on to the sofa*) We've got to tell them.

Adrian (*moving down behind the sofa*) There's nothing to worry about.

Mildred (*fiercely*) You don't understand. It wasn't Donald who killed them. It was me.

They all look at her in shock as the Lights fade and the scene ends

SCENE 2

The same. Ten minutes later

The curtains have been closed again and the door is closed. Mildred is huddled on the sofa, dabbing at her eyes with a crumpled handkerchief, a blanket around her shoulders. Jessica sits next to her, looking anxious and Adrian stands almost C, slightly above the sofa

After a moment, Diana enters from the kitchen carrying a tray holding four mugs of coffee. Crossing to the coffee table, she deposits the tray and Jessica at once picks up a mug and presses it into Mildred's hands.

*Diana takes two mugs, gives one to Adrian then moves to the armchair
and sits*

Jessica (*to Mildred, gently*) So what happened then?

Mildred (*dully*) He asked me to marry him. (*She sips at the coffee*) I
thought he was joking at first, but he meant it. He actually meant it. I
had to tell Donald, of course. I knew he wouldn't like it, but his wife
would never divorce him, and I had to think of my own future. It wasn't
till after we had married, I found I was expecting. Jack thought it was
his. A reward from God for taking in a homeless nineteen-year-old and
making an honest woman of her. He were turning the back bedroom
into a nursery months before she were due to arrive. (*Bitterly*) I should
have known it'd all go wrong. Like it says in the Bible ... "Be sure
your sins'll find you out". She didn't even look human.

Jessica (*shocked*) How awful.

Mildred She didn't live, of course. She couldn't have. And what made
it worse was him knowing I could never have another. There was too
much internal damage. It's that what finished him off. He'd never been
what you'd call a sociable man but he desperately wanted a family.

Diana (*helpfully*) Didn't you think of adoption?

Jessica glares at her

Mildred (*continuing*) For some reason, he thought what had happened
was his fault, and God was punishing him. Most of his free time,
he'd be on his hands and knees praying for forgiveness, and when
he wasn't doing that, he'd have his head in his Bible, looking for
answers. (*Bitterly*) Not that he ever found any. This (*she indicates the
farm*) went to rack and ruin, the hands all left, and I had to manage as
best as I could. If it hadn't been for Don helping out, now and then,
we'd have lost the lot.

Adrian Did you never consult a doctor?

Mildred (*disdainfully*) Oh, yes. I called in his doctor. I didn't have much
choice. But all he did was give him anti-depressants, sleeping pills
and tell him to get more exercise. (*Bitterly*) It were help he needed.
Psychiatric help.

Diana But surely the tablets helped?

Mildred They might have done if he'd taken them. He found more
comfort in a bottle of whiskey. Some nights he were so drunk he
couldn't climb the stairs to bed.

Diana (*surprised*) You told us he hardly drank.

Mildred (*with a bit of the old spark*) It's not summat you admit to
perfect strangers.

Jessica (*butting in*) But the murders, Millie? You haven't told us why you ...

Mildred (*nodding*) I'm coming to that. I spotted him one night. A week or so before he died. I was in the Land Rover, coming back from the supermarket ... and saw the lorry turning up Felstone Road. There were no mistaking it. Even in the moonlight, I could tell it were Jack's. I couldn't understand it. He'd not been off the farm in days. I thought there must be summat wrong, so I set off after him. It wasn't till he switched his headlights off and headed for Seddon's Marsh, I started to worry. I thought he were going to kill himself. I didn't know what to do at first ... call the police or go after him, but by the time I'd made my mind up, he were out of sight. When I finally caught up with him, he were lifting her out of the lorry. (*Bitterly*) His little bit on the side. They'd gone up there for sex like a couple of randy teenagers while I were flogging my guts out to keep us from starving. I wanted to kill him ... and her ... but then I realized I didn't have to do that. She were dead already.

Adrian (*surprised*) You mean he'd killed her? Your husband?

Mildred (*flatly*) Her and the rest of 'em. Five poor women who happened to in the wrong place at the wrong time. He'd wrung their necks like chickens and buried 'em in Seddon's marsh ...

Diana (*protesting*) But you told us you killed them.

Mildred (*tartly*) An' who else is to blame? If I'd had a normal baby, it would never have happened. If I'd told him it were Donald's baby, not his, we might have worked summat out. But I didn't. I kept my mouth shut, and let him think it were his fault. (*Bitterly*) It were me who sent him mad.

Jessica (*pleading*) No. No, Millie. You mustn't think that.

Mildred (*almost dreamily*) He started thinking God were speaking to him ... giving him messages. If folks weren't shaped in their maker's image, it were obvious they were spawn of the devil ... like our baby was ... and needed getting rid of. If he wanted God's forgiveness, he'd to scourge the land of anybody imperfect, an' show the devil that Jack McBride were doing The Lord's work. An' that's how it began. For ten years he'd been murdering poor unfortunates because God told him to, and I hadn't suspected a thing.

There is a slight pause as the others digest this

Adrian So what happened then? When he knew you'd found out.

Mildred Nothing happened. We just went on as usual.

Diana (*aghast*) Without telling the police?

Mildred An' what good would that have done? It wouldn't bring 'em back. An' as for him, he'd no idea that what he'd been doing was wrong? He were just following God's orders. (*Heavily*) But I knew I had to do something. I had to stop him killing. So one night, when he'd been drinking and passed out at the kitchen table, I got him into the tractor, drove it to the top field, and turned it over on top of him. He never knew a thing, and it all went down as a tragic accident caused by drunken driving.

Adrian And what about Caffrey? Did he know any of this?

Mildred (*shaking her head*) After the news got out, he offered to work here full time. He'd lost his job in Selwick, his wife had died and he wanted to make a fresh start. I'd only Gavin Purdie here at that time, and he were as much use as a toothless cat. No. He didn't suspect a thing.

Adrian (*quietly*) You realize I have to report this?

Jessica (*to Mildred*) Mr Brookes is a policeman.

Mildred (*tiredly*) Then he can make sure they'll not blame Donald. He were a good man, Donald Caffrey. I'll not have his name blackened for summat he knew nothing about.

Diana But what about the other woman? The one they found this morning? Who killed her?

Mildred I did. From the day they found the others, I'd been expecting them to turn up on the doorstep wi' evidence linking their deaths wi' Jack. Who knew what he'd left up there in the way of clues? He were too mad to be careful and it could have been anything. It's taken me ten years to build up the business again, and if they traced him back here I'd be finished. (*To Jessica*) She turned up twenty minutes after Don had gone to collect her, and told me her name. It were Etta Lipton.

Jessica looks at her in disbelief

She'd taken an earlier train, got off at Chellingford Junction by mistake and decided to walk here. It were the answer to everything. If the police found another body on the moor, there were no way they'd suspect Jack. He'd been dead for years. So I killed her, put her in the lorry with an old tarpaulin over her, and buried her near Mullen's Rock soon as the others had gone to bed.

Adrian Why Mullen's Rock?

Mildred (*drily*) I'd have thought that were obvious. Your lot were still digging around Seddon Marsh, and I needed to put her somewhere she'd be found quickly. That's why I left a bit of her dress showing. You don't see many poppies round Mullen's Rock.

Jessica (*still staring at Mildred*) And what about the ... injuries?

Mildred I hadn't much choice if I wanted 'em to think she'd been killed by the same man. She'd nothing wrong with her, you see, so I had to make 'em think she had. With her face gone, they'd just assume.

Diana (*horrified*) Oh, my God.

Adrian (*taking out his mobile phone*) I'd better call Tyson.

Jessica (*alarmed*) No.

Adrian turns upstage and punches out a number

Mildred (*gently*) It's all right, Jess. It's all in the open, now. Wi' Donald gone, I've nothing left to live for. I'll take the blame for everything. (*She forces a smile*) And ... it'll put a stop to his little game, won't it?

Jessica (*puzzled*) I'm sorry ?

Mildred (*in disgust*) Gavin Purdie. He must have seen me. The night I put her on the moor. I told him Donald had taken her to the station, but he's done nowt but drop hints and make insinuations for the last few weeks. I think he were building himself up to start blackmailing me, but he didn't dare risk it wi' Donald around.

Diana (*to Jessica*) I told you there was something wrong with him. I knew it the minute I met him.

Adrian (*into his mobile phone*) Tyson? It's DS Brookes. I'm still at McBride's Farm. Round at the cottage. You'd better get here. I think it'll make your day. (*He listens*) No. No. You need to hear it for yourself. But it does mean you can call off your team. The hunt's over. (*He ends the call*)

Mildred (*rising*) I'll be in the farmhouse.

Adrian I'd rather you waited here.

Mildred (*wearily*) There's things to do. The place won't run itself after I've gone. I need to write things down for whoever takes over. (*Drily*) You needn't worry. I won't be making a run for it. Not at my age.

Adrian Then someone had better go with you. Just to be on the safe side.

Diana (*bridling*) Well don't look at me. I'm not babysitting a murderess.

Jessica (*snapping*) Nobody asked you to.

Adrian (*firmly*) I was going to say that I'd accompany you.

Jessica (*rising*) It's all right. I'll do it.

Adrian (*shaking his head*) Out of the question.

Jessica Why's that? Do you think I'll attack her because she killed Etta?

Adrian (*surprised*) Of course not.

Jessica Then there's nothing to worry about, is there? I won't take my eyes off her till Inspector Tyson arrives. (*She takes Mildred's arm and leads her to the door*)

Adrian (*caught napping*) Now just a minute ...

Jessica (*with determination*) I'm going.

Jessica and Mildred exit

Diana (*with a theatrical shudder*) She's more nerve than I have. You wouldn't catch me being alone with a lunatic. (*Brightening*) But I could use it in the book, couldn't I? They wouldn't be able to stop me.

Adrian What book?

Diana I'm an author. True crimes. You might have read my Julia Wallace one?

Adrian shakes his head

(*Disappointed*) Oh. (*Brightly*) Well my next one's about the Chellingford murders. That's why I'm here. To do the research. I never dreamed I'd be in at the kill, so to speak. You couldn't buy that sort of publicity if you tried. (*Generously*) It'll be good for you, as well, won't it? (*Simpering*) I could even hint we were working together. (*Imagining it*) "Detective Sergeant Brookes praised the author's contribution in solving these appalling murders. Crimes which had baffled police for the past twenty years".

Adrian (*drily*) It's Tyson's case, actually. Nothing to do with me. And the time-span was a only a month. Until they found the bodies, they'd no idea a crime had been committed. And as for writing about it ...

Diana (*brightly*) I knew another detective called Brookes a few years ago. Well ... not exactly knew him. Knew *of* him. But he was only a constable.

Adrian (*moving over to close the door*) There's a lot of us about.

Diana He was married to a friend of my aunt.

Adrian (*uninterested*) Good for him.

Diana Ooooh. Do I detect a little bitterness?

Adrian (*frowning*) What?

Diana (*curious*) Are *you* married?

Adrian (*moving down* R) I am, actually. But we're living apart. Split up a few years back.

Diana (*archly*) I hope it wasn't your fault. Rebecca had an awful time with her husband.

Adrian freezes

(*Not noticing*) Used to beat her black and blue, according to Aunt Gerry.

Adrian (*turning to her*) Gerry?

Diana   Geraldine. Geraldine Lucas. She was Community Services Director in Marlock. Threw it all up one day and took off for Italy with Rebecca. We only found out where she was, when the email arrived.

Adrian   Must have been a surprise.

Diana   (*shrugging*) I don't know. Most people thought they were having an affair. But I've always thought she was trying to get Becky as far away from *him* as possible. They wouldn't believe it, you see. That he used to beat her up. (*Hotly*) He even tried to strangle her once, but being in the police force, managed to wriggle his way out of it.

Adrian   And how do *you* know about all this? It wasn't in the email.

Diana   (*agreeing*) No. It was in one of her letters. She wrote me every week when I was away at university. Keeping me up to date with what was happening back home. The psychopath, she used to call him. He'd even threatened her. (*Laughing*) I thought he'd killed them both when she vanished, but Sue convinced me I was being paranoid, and when the email came, I was glad I'd not made a fool of myself by kicking up a stink. (*Frowning*) But how do *you* know what was in the email? (*She looks at him and realizes*) Oh, my God. It's you, isn't it?

Adrian   (*warily*) What is?

Diana   (*pressing back in the chair*) The psychopath. You're Becky Brookes's husband.

Adrian   (*forcing a laugh*) Of course I'm not.

Diana   (*frightened*) You are. I can tell it by your face.

Adrian   (*amused*) Then you really should see an optician.

Diana   (*standing*) I never did believe it came from her. She was a coeliac. The last place on earth she'd have gone to was Italy. (*Horrified*) You *did* kill them, didn't you? (*She backs away* L)

Adrian   Don't be so stupid.

Diana   (*becoming hysterical*) You did. You *did*. You buried them somewhere, and sent that email to her office to put us all off the scent. That's why no one's heard from them since. They're dead.

Adrian   (*laughing*) It's easy to see you're a crime writer. You've got a great imagination.

Diana   (*edging towards the door*) We'll see what Inspector Tyson thinks when he/she arrives. I've still got the letters, you know. All of them.

Adrian   You really are making a fool of yourself. (*He moves towards her*)

Diana   (*dashing for the door and trying to open it*) Keep away from me.

Adrian grabs her from behind

Adrian   You've made a mistake.

Diana (*screaming*) Let go of me. Let go. (*She struggles*)

Adrian (*furiously*) Stop it, you stupid little bitch. (*He swings her round and his hands go to her neck. Squeezing*) I ... told ... you ... to ... stop ... it.

Diana struggles vainly then suddenly slumps. Panting heavily, Adrian releases his grip and she slides to the ground, dead

  (*Staring at her, horrified*) Oh, God. Oh, God.

Boris begins barking, and Jessica is heard, off

Jessica (*off, calling*) All right. All right. It's only me.

The barking stops. Adrian looks around in a panic, then grabbing hold of Diana's body he hastily drags her into the kitchen, emerges again and closes the door behind him. Hurrying to the sofa, he sits

  A moment later, Jessica enters

Adrian (*turning his head to see her*) What's happened? She's not taken off?

Jessica No, no. Of course not.

Adrian (*rising*) Then what are you doing back here? You're supposed to be keeping an eye on her till Tyson arrives.

Jessica I know. But she's in the kitchen, writing out instructions, and I had to talk to you. (*Glancing round*) Where's she gone?

Adrian Diana, you mean? God knows. She had a phone call and shot off like a greyhound. But couldn't it have waited? This whatever it is you want to talk about?

Jessica (*shaking her head*) It's got to be now. Before Inspector Tyson arrives. It's about Millie.

Adrian What about her?

Jessica (*moving down* R) I knew she was lying when she said she'd killed Etta. She couldn't possibly have done it. She couldn't kill anybody.

Adrian (*drily*) What about her husband?

Jessica (*sitting in the armchair*) That was different. I could understand that. You could hardly call it murder.

Adrian What would you call it, then? She rolled a bloody tractor on top of him.

Jessica But only to stop him killing again. You could hardly blame her for that. I'd call it justified murder.

Adrian A jury might disagree.

Jessica Well we'll cross that bridge when we come to it. For the minute, I need your advice.

Adrian Mine?

Jessica You're a policeman. You must know something about the law.

Adrian I know it's an ass ... according to Mr Bumble. But go on.

Jessica You'd better sit down.

He looks at her for a moment, then sits on the sofa

As I said ... I knew she was lying about killing Etta, and when I went back to the house with her, I managed to get the true story. There was no visitor on the day Etta vanished. She didn't turn up at the farmhouse, and Millie didn't kill her.

Adrian Then why ...

Jessica (*continuing*) The woman she buried on the moor had been there a week before the police even knew that Etta was missing.

Adrian (*frowning*) But you identified her.

Jessica I know. And I'll get to that later. But you need to know the rest. There was a guest at the farmhouse. A Frenchwoman. On a walking holiday. Apparently she had asthma. Rather a bad case of it, and had to use an inhaler quite a lot. The second night she stayed there, she didn't come down for breakfast, so Millie went up to see if anything was wrong and found her dead on the bedroom floor. She almost called the police, but had second thoughts when she imagined what it could lead to. So she dressed her and did what she told us she did. Buried her up on the moor. And the rest of it, you know.

Adrian So why admit to killing Mrs Lipton?

Jessica (*taking a deep breath*) Because she thought I'd killed her.

Adrian (*incredulously*) You?

Jessica (*nodding*) I'd told her a lot about Etta. How we'd met. The accident that killed her husband. How she'd been cheated out of his insurance and had to move away. Where she lived now ... and how she was leaving me all she had left in her will. Not that her house was worth much. The sale of it would just about have settled the mortgage. But her life insurance was over half a million.

Adrian (*shaking his head*) I don't buy it. If she knew the body she'd buried wasn't Etta Lipton, why should she think you'd killed the real one?

Jessica Because she knew I hadn't two pennies to call my own. I owed her four months rent on this place, and there wasn't a hope she'd get it unless I somehow inherited. When I came back from identifying the fake Etta, she really thought it was her, till I mentioned the injuries and the dress with red poppies. It was then that she realized I was lying.

And why? Because I was so desperate to get my hands on Etta's life insurance, I'd purposely identified the wrong body.

Adrian But how could you have killed her? You were here all day. Waiting for her to arrive.

Jessica They'd only my word I was expecting her here. I could have killed her days before and buried her almost anywhere.

Adrian And why would she want to take the blame for something she thought you'd done? Don't say it was for four month's rent arrears.

Jessica I think she felt sorry for me. We were birds of a feather. Both of us killing out of desperation. Now she'd confessed to killing her husband, what difference would a second murder make?

Adrian So what's the problem? If she didn't kill this Frenchwoman ... and the post mortem'll easily confirm that ... she'll still face charges for one murder, and for attempting to pervert the course of justice.

Jessica (*flatly*) And what about me?

Adrian (*frowning*) What about you? You haven't killed anyone.

Jessica (*rising*) But I have. I killed Etta Lipton. (*She turns away* R)

Adrian reacts

The only trouble is, they'll never find her body. She *had* to die, you see. So I could inherit. (*She moves upstage*) But I couldn't work out how to do it. Not at first. (*She moves behind the easy chair*) Since she'd moved to Tamstock, Etta had kept herself to herself. The house was outside the village, with no close neighbours, so no one really got to know her. She was bitter, angry, and the little money she'd left was fast running out. The only glimmer of light was her life insurance ... but to claim it, she'd have to be dead. And that's where I came in. (*She stops*)

Adrian (*after a moment*) Go on.

Jessica She found this place in one of the newspapers. Came over to see it and rented it the same day in the name of Jessica Scanlon. (*She pauses*) I moved in the following week.

Adrian (*realizing*) You mean ...?

Jessica Exactly. Jessica Scanlon and Etta Lipton are one and the same person.

Adrian stares at her

It's why I knew neither Millie or Donald had killed her. From the day I moved in here, Etta was dead. Nobody knew that, of course. I went back to Tamstock every week to pay bills and answer letters, etcetera, and keep up the illusion she was still in residence. But for the past four years, I've been consolidating my new identity as watercolour artist Jessica Scanlon and waiting for a chance to hit back at the bastards who cheated me out of John's insurance.

Adrian So ... what were you planning?

Jessica (*tiredly*) I'd have thought that was obvious. As Margaretta Lipton, I made out a will leaving everything I owned to my friend Jessica Scanlon, then sat back and waited for an unidentified body to turn up so I could claim it was hers, and collect the money.

Adrian (*amused*) Do you know how ridiculous that sounds? Contrary to belief, we don't make a habit of digging up unidentifiable bodies on a regular basis.

Jessica (*heavily*) So I discovered. But I was absolutely desperate by the time they discovered the bodies on the moor, and decided to take a chance. No one had mentioned how long they'd been up there, just that they could only identify two of them, so I reported Etta missing, hoping they'd think she was one of the other victims.

Adrian But when you realized your mistake, it was too late to retract?

Jessica (*nodding*) When they told me they'd found another body ... a much more recent one ... I could have died of relief. I'd have identified anyone as Etta to pull myself out of the hole I'd dug. I just never expected her to be so ... mutilated. I almost had a breakdown.

Adrian (*curiously*) So why are you telling me all this?

Jessica Because Millie insists she's going to tell Inspector Tyson the same story she told us, and I can't let her be accused of a murder that never took place.

Adrian Even if your planned insurance scam has to come to light?

Jessica (*nodding*) It was a mad idea, anyway. It probably wouldn't have worked. But ... (*hesitating*)... what will happen to me? Will I be prosecuted?

Adrian (*hesitating*) It all depends. There'll be charges of course. Wasting police time, for a start. But if you haven't already made a claim, you can hardly be charged with actual fraud. I'd suggest you get yourself a good solicitor.

Jessica (*smiling weakly and nodding*) I'll get back to Millie, then. She'll be wondering where I am.

As she turns to the door, there is the sound of a distant gunshot. Adrian stands and they look at each other

(*Realizing*) Millie. (*To Adrian; horrified*) I think she's shot herself. (*She rushes to the door and opens it*)

Adrian (*fumbling for his mobile phone*) I'll call an ambulance.

Jessica hurries out and R

Jessica (*screaming; off*) Millie.

Boris begins barking furiously

> *Adrian hurries to the kitchen door, opens it and exits. A moment later, he backs out again, apparently dragging Diana's body*

Jessica rushes back in breathlessly and takes in the sight

Oh.

Adrian releases Diana's hands and straightens, turning to Jessica in horror. She looks past him, into the kitchen and steps back

Adrian (*hastily*) It was an accident.
Jessica (*staring into the kitchen*) Diana?
Adrian She fell. And hit her head.
Jessica (*numbly*) You said she'd gone.
Adrian I know. But if you'll let me explain ... (*He moves towards her*)
Jessica (*still confused*) Is she dead?
Adrian (*savagely*) Of course she's dead, you brainless bitch. (*He grabs her wrist*) She was going to tell Tyson.
Jessica (*protesting*) You're hurting me. (*She attempts to free herself*)
Adrian (*grimly*) Why the hell did you come back? Two more minutes, I'd have had her out of here.
Jessica (*stammering*) The first aid box. I thought I'd better ...

He thrusts her away R *and she staggers back rubbing at her wrist*

Adrian (*almost to himself; furiously*) All this time. All this time and no one suspected a thing. Then she comes along, and screws up everything.

Boris stops barking

Jessica (*still in shock*) I don't know what you're talking about.
Adrian (*savagely*) Do you know what the odds are? Against her being here and knowing who I was? (*Almost whispering*) It must be billions. Billions to one. (*Brightening*) But I've beaten them, haven't I? I've beaten the odds.
Jessica (*nervously*) What are you saying?

Adrian (*ignoring this*) I didn't know, did I? That the bitch had a niece. She never mentioned it, you see? She just said I'd never see Becky again. They were going someplace I'd never find her. (*Incredulously*) Well I couldn't have that, could I? She was my property. (*Growing angry*) Mine. She belonged to me. (*Calmly*) They were having tea when I went to her house. Calmly drinking tea ... (*bitterly*) with their bags already packed, and waiting for a taxi. (*Flatly*) So I killed them. (*His voice rises*) Right there in her high-tech, hand-crafted, over-priced, sodding foreign kitchen, with a cheap Ikea *meat tenderiser*. (*Calmly*) Half an hour later, we were on our way to Chellingford.

Jessica (*baffled*) Who were?

Adrian (*savagely*) Aren't you listening? (*Indicating the kitchen*) Her bloody Aunt Geraldine and my two-faced lying wife. (*Calmly*) I knew they'd never be looked for here ... eighty miles away from where they'd last been seen ... and I knew the moor like the back of my hand. So I buried them in Seddon's Marsh and left them to rot, while *I* went back and acted out the role of a cuckolded husband to anyone who'd listen. (*He laughs in disbelief*) People are such fools. They'll believe anything if they want to. It's been four years now, and they still think the little turtle-doves are living it up in Milan.

Jessica (*regarding him in horror*) And what about Laura? Your sister?

Adrian (*sneering*) You really are stupid, aren't you? There never was a sister. She was just an excuse to explain what I was doing in this area.

Jessica (*hesitantly*) Which *was*?

Adrian (*perching on the R arm of the easy chair*) When they found those bodies in Seddon's Marsh, I nearly had a heart attack. Not because they'd anything to do with me, but because I knew the way the force worked. For the next few days they'd be searching for others, and I couldn't take the chance of them stumbling across the two I'd buried there. So I came up here on the pretext of looking for a missing sister and moved them. (*Grimly*) But thanks to you, your little insurance scam, and Millie McBride, you drew their attention away from the Marsh and over to Mullen's Rock ... exactly where I'd just re-buried them. (*Amused*) I couldn't believe it. I'd taken every precaution I could think of, and now I was back where I started. And to make matters worse, that old idiot Caffrey remembered me. It was only a matter of time before he'd also remember I didn't *have* a sister, and blow my story apart, so I'd no choice but to shut him up before he opened his mouth.

Jessica (*horrified*) You mean ——

Adrian (*sneering*) Of course I *mean*. (*He rises sharply and moves towards her*)

Jessica retreats down R. *He stops, behind the sofa*

He was so busy avoiding puddles, he'd no idea I was there till I hit him with the shovel. (*Smugly*) I had him hanging in the barn before he'd time to come round.

Jessica But you said you'd just arrived. Because of the message.

Adrian (*smiling*) Which I'd phoned through myself, to give me an alibi. All bases covered, you see? (*Snarling*) Then *she* (*he indicates the kitchen with his head*) had to stick her nose in. Gerry Paige's niece. (*In disbelief*) Of all the places in the world she could have been, she turns up here. I thought I was going mad.

Jessica (*stunned*) You *are* mad. Stark, staring mad.

Adrian (*ignoring this*) He was right, wasn't he? The man who said it. (*In a dreamy tone*) Oh, what a tangled web we weave, when first we practice to deceive. (*He smiles at her strangely*) And we've all been practicing, haven't we? You ... me ... and Mrs B. (*He giggles*) Whoops. I'm a poet, and didn't know it. (*He giggles*)

Jessica makes a dash for the door, but Adrian swiftly prevents this by stepping into her path

(*Playfully*) Naughty, naughty. Mustn't leave the party now it's in full swing.

Jessica (*backing away*) Millie. I've got to see to Millie.

Adrian (*lightly*) I don't think so. Quite a determined woman, our Mrs McBride. If she *has* shot herself, I'm sure she's made a very good job of it. After all ... practice makes perfect, and as she's already admitted to one murder, three more will hardly come as a surprise.

Jessica (*blankly*) Three?

Adrian (*indicating Diana*) Her ... Caffrey ... and you, of course.

Jessica They'll never believe that.

Adrian Oh, they will. Especially with me to back it up. You were having an affair with Caffrey, you see, and when she found out, it tipped her over the edge again.

Jessica (*in disbelief*) But that's ridiculous. He was old enough to be my father.

Adrian (*shrugging*) So maybe she imagined it? Who knows what goes through a deranged woman's mind? But she killed him by stringing him up in the barn, and strangled *you* for trying to steal him away from her.

Jessica And what about Diana?

Adrian (*easily*) Came round here to see if you were still all right, caught her red-handed, and paid the price. When I got worried and followed her, Mrs M realized the game was up, confessed to everything, then gave me the slip and killed herself. (*He sighs*) A sad, sad ending to a tragic story. (*Smiling*) And now I'd better get on with it before Tyson arrives. Wouldn't do to find you still alive, would it?

He advances towards her and she retreats

(*Conversationally*) You can scream if you like ... but no one's going to hear you.

Rhoda appears in the doorway

Rhoda I think they might.

Adrian turns in shock, and Jessica sags with relief

(*Entering*) And you won't get away with it, *this* time. Oh, yes. I know about Becky. I know you killed her and hid the body, but no one would listen to *me*. I was just an alcoholic bag-lady who hardly knew what day it was. (*Grimly*) But if they wouldn't listen to me, I was going to make sure justice was done, even if I'd to kill you myself.
Adrian (*puzzled*) Who are you?
Rhoda (*smiling coldly*) You've no idea, have you? I doubt you even knew I existed. Not that I'm surprised. I ceased to be part of her life when the demon drink got his claws into me. From middle class scientist to down-and-out bag-lady in one fell swoop.
Adrian (*realizing*) Becky's mother? But she said you were dead.
Rhoda (*sardonically*) I'm sure she did. We hadn't spoken in years, but I still loved her, despite everything, and when I heard the nurses talking ——
Adrian (*puzzled*) Nurses?
Rhoda I'd developed pneumonia and collapsed in the park. Someone found me there and took me to hospital. I don't know how she found out, but Becky came to see me. Told me all about you. How unhappy she was, how you ill-treated her, broke her bones and tried to strangle her. Not that I heard, of course; I was still unconscious. But the nurses did. When I finally came round, I overheard them talking. They'd no idea I was listening or they'd have been more discreet, but the minute the hospital discharged me, I went to your house to hear it for myself.
Adrian (*incredulously*) You've been in my house?
Rhoda (*shaking her head*) There was no one at home. But that's when I found out she'd left you. A neighbour told me she'd run away to Italy

with her lesbian lover. (*Scornfully*) Lesbian lover. (*In disbelief*) How could anyone believe that? (*Coldly*) And then I saw it. In the charity shop. The little jewelled watch her father gave her shortly before he died. There was no mistaking it. I'd seen it a thousand times and knew she'd *never* have gone away leaving that behind, let alone donated it to charity. That's when I realized I'd never see her again. You'd killed her.

Adrian (*sneering*) So you're the drunken old bat who tried to grass me up four years ago and got herself tossed out?

Rhoda (*calmly*) Guilty as charged. But from that day on, I've never touched another drop. I sobered up, re-joined the normal world, found myself a job, and promised myself I'd discover where you'd hidden her body and have you jailed for the rest of your life. (*She moves slightly down* L) That's how I came to be here. I'd been following you around for the last few years, but a trip to Chellingford was something new. Why would a thug like you be interested in open countryside? It was only when I remembered those bodies being found that I made the connection. You'd buried her here, and were scared they'd find Becky as well.

Adrian (*dismissively*) You don't know what you're talking about.

Rhoda (*mildly*) Don't I? For the last few days, you've hardly taken a breath without me knowing you've done it. I only lost you the other night when you slipped out after dinner and vanished for the next few hours. But I knew you'd been up to something. You had a smug, self-satisfied look on your face at breakfast that made me want to scream. (*She takes a deep breath*) When nothing else happened for the next few days, I was feeling pretty dejected, but when I followed you here this morning, I made a fortunate mistake. I thought you were booking in and did the same myself. By the time I found out you hadn't, you were gone again and I'd no idea where. Imagine my relief when I went for a walk to decide what to do and saw you heading across the moor in the direction of Mullen's Rock. If it hadn't been for the storm breaking, I'd have followed you again ... but as it's turned out, there was no need. By staying here, I now know what I wanted to know. (*With grim satisfaction*) And it's the end of the line for you.

Jessica (*sinking onto the sofa*) Thank God you came back in time. But why?

Rhoda (*moving further down* L) I noticed his car as we left. Tucked away as though he was trying to hide it. And as he was supposed to have left some time ago, I got suspicious. First chance I had, I turned the car round and came back. We arrived just in time to hear the gunshot.

Jessica (*fearfully*) Is she ... ?

Rhoda (*nodding*) I'm sorry.

Jessica slumps

I was on my way here to see if you were safe, then saw the open door and heard his voice. He's quite mad, you know. I've suspected it for years. But it's all over now. Susan's calling the police, and as soon as they arrive, he'll be locked away for good.

Adrian (*sneering*) By the time they get here, I'll be halfway down the motorway. And after that ... (*He spreads his hands expressively*) Who knows? (*He grins*) As I said earlier ... all bases covered.

Jessica and Rhoda look uncertain

(*Easily*) I'm not a policeman for nothing. There was always the possibility I could be found out, no matter how unlikely it seemed. So I made arrangements for a quick departure if the need ever did arise. (*Smirking*) Once I'm away from here, they won't have a clue where to look for me.

Rhoda (*drily*) And you think we're going to let you go?

Adrian (*smirking*) Do you think you can stop me? (*He puts his hand in his pocket and takes out a flick-knife*)

As Adrian opens the knife, Rhoda and Jessica react

Gavin appears in the doorway, carrying an ancient-looking sickle

Gavin (*glaring at him*) P'raps they can't. But I can. (*He wields the sickle*)

Adrian reacts as Gavin enters

Adrian (*scornfully*) Don't be so stupid. Put it down and get out of the way.

Gavin (*grimly*) Going to try an' make me? (*He advances on him*)

Adrian (*backing away*) I'm warning you. I'll carve you apart like a turkey. (*He brandishes the knife*)

Gavin Got to get near me, first.

Adrian rushes at Gavin, but Gavin parries the knife with a vicious swipe of the sickle and Adrian hastily retreats

Reckon I could take that hand o' yours straight off with a swipe of old Betsy. And you'm not going nowhere till p'lice arrives.

Adrian (*wildly*) You bloody maniac. They'll be here any minute.

Inspector Tyson appears in the doorway

Tyson (*mildly*) We're here right now, actually. (*He enters the room*)

Sergeant Morley appears in the doorway

Adrian (*dropping the knife*) Thank God for that. He was going to kill me.
Tyson (*mildly*) *Was* he, indeed? (*Moving* c) And why was that, I wonder?
Adrian (*relaxing*) I'd found out the truth. About the moor killings. They were all done here. By the McBrides and Donald Caffrey. They buried them all over the place. Seddon's Marsh, Mullen's Rock ... They've been at it for years.
Tyson (*frowning*) I see.
Rhoda Don't listen to him, Inspector. He killed my daughter, Rebecca, her friend, Mrs Paige, and Diana Wishart, Mrs Paige's niece. You'll find her body through there. (*She indicates the kitchen*)

Sergeant Morley moves to the kitchen door, looks inside, turns and nods to Tyson

Jessica (*blurting*) And he also killed Donald Caffrey.

Adrian gives a disbelieving laugh

Tyson (*mildly*) Did he really? And you can prove this, can you?
Jessica (*protesting*) He's just admitted it.
Tyson (*seriously*) In that case, I'd better arrest him. Can't have a murderer running round loose, can we?

Sergeant Morley gets a notepad and pen out and stands poised

(*To Adrian*) Adrian George Brookes, I'm arresting you for the murders of ...
Adrian (*in alarmed amusement*) Just a minute. Just a minute. You can't arrest *me*. Not on the word of a crazy old bag-lady and a would-be insurance swindler.
Tyson (*reasonably*) Well, of course I can't. You know the law as well as I do. What I'm arresting you for, are the murders of ——
Adrian (*angrily*) I haven't murdered anybody. Why don't you listen to me? What's wrong with you? It's them who killed the woman in there. They were taking her up to the moor when I walked in on them. I'd nothing to do with it. I haven't killed anyone.

Tyson (*mildly*) Then could you explain what your warrant card was doing beneath the bodies of two females we recovered from the moor about half an hour ago?

Jessica, Gavin and Rhoda react

Adrian (*shaken*) I haven't a clue. (*Hastily*) I lost it a few days ago. It must have been planted there. It's years since I've been near Mullen's Rock.

Tyson (*mildly*) And who mentioned that, I wonder? *I* merely said we'd found them on the moor.

Adrian (*angrily*) You're fitting me up, you snotty-nosed bastard. (*He lunges at Tyson and attempts to strangle him/her*) I'll bloody well kill you.

Sergeant Morley rapidly grabs Adrian and frees Tyson after a struggle

(*Struggling wildly*) Let go of me. Let go.

Tyson Adrian George Brookes, I'm arresting you for the murders of Rebecca Joan Brookes and Geraldine Paige —

Adrian (*angrily*) No.

Tyson You do not have to say anything —

Adrian (*struggling wildly*) No.

The others freeze in position. The Lights begin to dim and fade to a black-out

Tyson — but it may harm your defence —

Adrian (*screaming madly*) Noooooooooooo.

Tyson — if you do not mention, when questioned, something which you later rely on in court.

Adrian (*sinking to his knees and moaning*) No, no, no, no, no.

Tyson Anything you do say, may be given in evidence.

CURTAIN

FURNITURE AND PROPERTY LIST

ACT I

SCENE 1

On stage: Two long windows
Stable-door with iron fittings and connecting bolt
Small, leaded windowed porch
Heavy looking drapes on wooden poles (at windows)
Oak cabinet with a set of drawers
Oak cabinet. *On it*: drinks bottles and assorted glassware
Flower bowls, vases, knick-knacks etc. (on cabinets)
Doorless opening with glimpse of narrow staircase
Welsh dresser. *On it*: large dinner service
Door leading to the kitchen
Large 1930s fireplace. *On it*: various objects
Framed portrait of elderly Victorian man
Bookcase. *On it*: assorted books and games
Rectangular table. *On it*: small television
Magazine rack
Comfortable-looking sofa
Matching armchair
Small occasional table. *On it*: table lamp, hard-backed book, reading glasses
Various framed pictures on walls
Light switches by main door and at foot of stairs

Off stage: Brown envelope containing studio photograph of a young woman (**Adrian**)
Double-barrelled shotgun (**Mildred**)
Two mugs of tea (**Mildred**)
Mug of tea (**Donald**)
Cloth (**Mildred**)

SCENE 2

Strike: Mugs

Off stage: Wheeled suitcase (**Susan**)
Shopping bag bulging with items (**Mildred**)
Tray holding four cups and saucers, milk jug, teapot, sugar bowl and spoons (**Jessica**)

ACT II

Scene 1

Strike: Tray with tea things

Set: Curtains open

Off stage: Small wicker basket covered with a cloth (**Gavin**)
Glass of orange juice (**Jessica**)

Personal: **Morley**: notebook and pen
Tyson: mobile phone (in pocket)

Scene 2

Set: Curtains closed
Door closed

Off stage: Tray holding four mugs of coffee (**Diana**)
Ancient looking sickle (**Gavin**)

Personal: **Mildred**: handkerchief, blanket
Adrian: mobile phone, flick knife (in pocket)

LIGHTING PLOT

Practical fittings required: ceiling lights in living-room, light in kitchen 1 interior, the same throughout

ACT I, SCENE 1

To open: Brilliant sunshine on interior

| Cue 1 | **Gavin** smiles knowingly | (Page 17) |
| | *Lights slowly fade* | |

ACT I, SCENE 2

To open: Overcast skies on interior, getting darker throughout the scene

| Cue 2 | **Jessica** switches on lights | (Page 22) |
| | *Ceiling lights on* | |

| Cue 3 | **Jessica** crosses to the kitchen and exits | (Page 26) |
| | *Kitchen light on* | |

| Cue 4 | **Mildred**: "... and see you later." | (Page 35) |
| | *Flash of lightning* | |

ACT II, SCENE 1

To open: Ceiling lights on, gloomy daylight outside

| Cue 5 | **Mildred**: "It was me." | (Page 53) |
| | *Lights fade* | |

ACT II, SCENE 2

To open: Ceiling lights on

No cues

EFFECTS PLOT

ACT I

Cue 13   **Jessica**: "It's only me."   (Page 60)
              Barking stops

Cue 14   **Jessica**: "She'll be wondering where I am."   (Page 63)
              Distant gunshot

Cue 15   **Jessica**: "Millie."   (Page 64)
              Furious dog barking

Cue 16   **Adrian**: "... and screws up everything."   (Page 64)
              Barking stops